Pavan Gill's book addresses two of the most pressing issues of our time: inequality and human security. Her integration of poetry into an insightful and well-researched work on ecological biodiversity and environmental harmony in India is both creative and original.

She excelled as one of my students at Royal Roads University, and I am encouraged by her contribution to this field of study.

Professor Gordon Smith
-Executive Director of the Centre for Global Studies
-Distinguished Fellow at the Centre for international
Governance Innovation (CIGI), and Adjunct Professor
of Political Science and Public Administration at the
University of Victoria

Nature's Verse is a quantum leap re-defined. So far removed in research and presentation from the *Lotus of the Lake* presentation yet ever so from the heart and pristine Pavan in every line and every thought.

"Would I were steadfast as thou art" Shakespeare would have said of you and I reiterate it now. You have never for one moment strayed from the path that you wandered on to so many years ago. And with you, your messages ring loud and true. And as you quoted from Ghandi "truth is God..." so then are your messages those that I believe God would want us to hear.

Congratulations on such a brilliant compilation of history, family involvement, the humanity "enigma" and where the world is at. It conjures an awareness which we find easier to embrace through the stark reality presented in your research that in turn is followed by the gentleness of your poetry which becomes the "yin and yang" of life, allowing the "light" to take away the "darkness" that surrounds us.

Davide Cottone

Author of Diary of a Devoted Poet

M.A.App.Ling., B.Ed., Dip.Teach., Cert.Ed

Nature's VERSE

Expanding Solar Energy Access Across the Globe to Promote Equality, Natural Energy and Sustainable Development in Underprivileged Areas

GURPAVAN KAUR GILL

WESTBOW
P R E S S
A DIVISION OF THOMAS NELSON

WestBow Press books may be ordered through booksellers or by contacting:

WestBow Press
A Division of Thomas Nelson
1663 Liberty Drive
Bloomington, IN 47403
www.westbowpress.com
1-(866) 928-1240

ISBN: 978-1-4497-4877-7 (sc)
ISBN: 978-1-4908-0392-0 (e)

Library of Congress Control Number: 2012907593

Printed in the United States of America

WestBow Press rev. date: 10/18/2013

Contents

Acknowledgments

I would like to thank our Creator by whom the fabric of our universe has been weaved in a perfection we can only begin to fathom. He has intricately stitched life's hem, the galaxies, nebulas, our majestic planet and all ethereal realms together in an unwavering interdependence. I would also like to thank nature for its majesty, wonder and patience, inspiring me in every breath of life.

Further, I would like to thank all of my friends from India, China, Africa, Thailand and all parts of the world that have inspired me to continue my work due to the love they have within their hearts. Thank you.

I would like to acknowledge and thank my grandfather, Parmanand Singh, for his resilience and his integrity in devoting his life to social welfare and human rights while raised in a hierarchical society. I wish to thank my mother for her constant care, attention and support and my father for guiding me and always believing in my dreams. I would also like to thank my brother and sister for their support and strength. Further, I want to thank my Professors and fellow graduates in the Human Security and Peace building program at Royal Roads University. They have helped me develop sound goals and encouraged me to live for what I believe in. Through their example and their dedication to Human Security, the world is moving towards a better future. I would like to thank Dr. Natalee Popadiuk for reviewing my manuscript and for her wisdom, knowledge and leadership and for being a wonderful Professor, role model and friend. I would also like to thank Davide Cottone for his analysis of this book and Vanessa Louise Goodall for contributing research data on food security and editing the manuscript through to publication.

Foreword

Pavan Gill articulately and passionately creates a detailed picture of what is required to change the lives of people in India. She brings us into her personal life by honouring her grandfather, Parmanand Singh, and his quest to bring peace, equality, and respect to the lower classes, the "untouchables," of his homeland. Even after being imprisoned for 14 years for social justice work that was deemed subversive, he continued to act on his principles and peacefully work toward social change. Decades later, Pavan finds her way back to the home of her grandfather with a vision to make real and measurable changes for the poorest and most vulnerable children and families living there – the Dalith or "untouchables."

In her writing, Pavan calls upon us to consider a new paradigm that could make a difference in the world. What would it mean for us to reflect upon our taken-for-granted assumptions and actions that impact our natural world, food security, and international peace? What would it mean for us to contemplate that child labour in India might be the reason we can buy beautiful carpets or clothing at reasonable prices? What would it mean for nations to divert monies slated for war, death, and destruction, and instead, feed people nutritious food, educate children to become leaders with integrity, and harness green technologies to bring energy and light to rural communities?

In the opening chapters, Pavan provides compelling evidence about the caste system, economic needs, the environment, and energy requirements. Her impassioned research helps us to better understand the intricacies of the situation – the history, traditions, politics, and ongoing complexities. Comparisons to other nations, like China and Brazil, who have experienced similar crises of poverty and a lack of education for the poor contextualizes the efforts, or lack thereof, and points to possible alternative solutions. The message is clear: change is possible in India, but governments must act with integrity and create solutions that can be implemented and sustained.

In addition to the facts, Pavan opens her heart and soul to the people, the geography, and the spiritual practices through evocative poems, drawings, and photographs. She shares her passion and compassion for the people, nature, and all the things that make us human in this world. Her words and images supersede the intellectual, and instead stir our emotions, our humanity. Pavan demonstrates the interconnectedness of life and gracefully provides sustenance to knowledge and allows us to experience the beauty and the tragedy of many Indian people today.

Pavan also writes from her own internship experiences working for the Canadian International Development Agency (CIDA) in India on the slum dwellers project and rural development. She collected data from stakeholders and reached the conclusion that more needed to be done to assist the Dalith people, the "untouchables," to provide for their most basic needs – education, healthcare, belonging. As the founder of the Lotus Foundation for Children, Pavan steadfastly continues to bring the plight of the Dalith people into the world's awareness, and works diligently to change their lives right where they live. I am honoured to be able to support Pavan in her quest for social justice in some small way, and amazed at the work that she has accomplished thus far. Like her grandfather, Pavan has the knowledge and the passion to change the lives of the poorest and most vulnerable amongst us.

> "At the end of life we will not be judged by how many diplomas we have received, how much money we have made, how many great things we have done. We will be judged by 'I was hungry and you gave me to eat, I was naked and you clothed me, I was homeless and you took me in.' Hungry not only for bread - but hungry for love. Naked not only for clothing - but naked for human dignity and respect. Homeless not only for want of a room of bricks - but homeless because of rejection."

Mother Teresa

Dr. Natalee Popadiuk
Professor in the Department of
Counselling Psychology
University of Victoria

Genesis

In the beginning God created the heavens and the earth. Now the earth was formless and empty, darkness was over the surface of the deep, and the Spirit of God was hovering over the waters. And God said, "Let there be light," and there was light. God saw that the light was good, and he separated the light from the darkness.[1]

Part 1

We are One

jaanahu joth n pooshhahu jaathee aagai jaath n hae ||1||
rehaao ||[2]
Recognize the Lord's Light within all, and do not consider social class or status; there are no classes or castes in the world hereafter. ||1||Pause||

manas ki jat sabhe eke paihcanbo[3]
Recognise all of mankind as a single caste of humanity.

neh baran baran neh kuleh kul ||[4]
You have no caste or social class.

Introduction

It was during the period of British occupancy in India that my grandfather decided to speak out against the civil inconsistencies and the harsh political, socio-economic and religious disparities of the time. The inequalities during the mid 1900s were notably catastrophic. The British were drawing lines through the land, classifying and categorizing people, as if playing hopscotch on a sub-continent. In the process of their game, the caste system was strengthened, as were religious divides. Political power was taken away from the majority of the population during most of the British reign and leadership was left in the hands of the affluent classes who were unfamiliar with the living conditions endured by millions of Indians. This imbalance of state control endures today causing great clashes among the "haves" and the "have nots."

My grandfather, Parmanand Singh, also known as "Bapu Ji" was born during this time of turmoil, in 1913, in a large village called Boparai Khurd, Punjab. He dedicated the majority of his life to the quest for freedom from British occupancy in India. He spent most of his life initiating social change by demanding justice and equality through group movements, writing and public opposition to the state in a country divided and diminished by superficial measures such as wealth and caste. He spent fourteen years in prison in the fight for the equality of oppressed individuals. After 1947, he began raising awareness about the rights and freedoms of oppressed and vulnerable members of Indian society. He stood up for individuals who had no rights yet who contributed extensively to almost every sector of civil life. He went to prison because he demanded the liberation and respectful treatment of individuals from lower socio-economic backgrounds or the "lower" castes of India.

He dreamt of an India where all people are treated as equals and respected as humans—not **caste in the shadows**. And although he helped raise awareness and promoted voting rights among all castes in the villages of Punjab, due to rigid hierarchies and prejudiced decision making processes inherent in Indian politics, his journey lives on today as does the struggle among Daliths to be accepted as equal members of society. Equality has not yet been achieved in the absence of a set of universal human rights.

As a socialist my Grandfather had an idealistic point of view; he believed that Indian economic growth and resource distribution should be centralized and equally re-distributed throughout India. He believed too, with an iron will, that in order for India and its entire population to prosper, a socialist agenda was required. To him, democratic socialism could provide adequate food, shelter and employment for families of all classes and bridge the vast divides between the affluent and lower classes—inviting a state of equilibrium and standardized human development across India. Ultimately, he believed that socialism would help to dissolve the caste system and give rise to a more meritocratic society.

During his childhood, Bapu witnessed countless instances in which members of the under classes were disrespected, misjudged and outcaste from civil liberties, social exchanges and community events in the villages of Punjab. These experiences were common throughout every state in India; even today Daliths are treated as shadows in their own societies due to economic constraints. Much to the surprise of other villagers, my grandfather ate from the same plate as his friend, who was a Dalith in his village. Contrarily, most villagers would not have ventured to touch the plate handled by an "untouchable" as they are considered "unhygienic" based on the nature of their work and labour—street cleaning, leather tanning, and brick making.

In another experience, my grandfather witnessed a Dalith child bringing fresh milk for a prayer ceremony to the village school. The high priest, a Sikh, who my Grandfather greatly respected because of his wisdom and knowledge, refused to accept the offering of milk from the Dalith child for the ceremony. Instead, he spilled the milk in front of several young students on school grounds, deeming it impure. The child who brought the milk watched shamefully as the priest disrespected his entire household in an instant without sound reason. The milk he brought was from the same village and from the same cows as any other abode in the village. Yet, because of an illogical and scientifically inaccurate assumption or paradigm created by the misinterpretation of holy texts, this young child and his caste were shunned—generations have been displaced by such misconceptions.

It was Bapu's great dream to see India thrive as an elevated nation—one in which people are judged by the labour of their ancestors, the work of their hands, their personal merit, their words, their thoughts, and values—not their social class or the colour of their skin. For over sixty years he toiled to bring about a movement of solidarity, cooperation and mutual respect in a country torn by prejudice and caste distinction.

When Bapu visited Canada for the first time, I was seven years old. At that time, I could not clearly conceive what he and his colleagues were fighting for as I did not fully understand the concept of socialism. Although I knew it was radically different from the ideology of the time—I sensed that their stance was revolutionary and that political turmoil in India required a change in order for peace and order to prevail. Bapu would often organize committee meetings in our small abode on East 13th Avenue in East Vancouver in the late 1980s. The discussions about the socialist agenda, power and politics in India would often become highly political and rigidly controversial—afterall the future of India was at stake. However, through all of the discussions, the heated debates, the committee meetings, and political gatherings my grandfather never lost his temper. There existed a determination in the eyes of my grandfather that never once dimmed or weakened. He believed in the cause of social justice in an honest and sincere manner. And his perseverance helped him lead his villagers to vote in the democratic election without fear of government retaliation. I remember, Bapu was never resentful that change was slow to grow in India—always calm, sure and strong. It is his determination that I recall and use as my strength today.

The Purpose of this Book

India is the soul of the world—where spirituality and art intertwine with the ethereal realms in a way that cannot be described by mere words, only experienced. The creative genius presented by the individuals in this magnificent country is utterly remarkable and infinitely limitless. The brilliant minds of India have given rise to poetry, music, dance and drama that is timeless and often universally acclaimed. India has produced poets such as, Rabrinath Tagore and Amrita Pritham, social activists such as, Mahatma Gandhi, spiritual leaders such as, the Buddha and Mai Bhago, musical geniuses such as A.R. Rehman and Lata Mangashkar, and timeless art and architecture including the Taj Mahal, Harimandir Sahib, Birla Mandir and the B'hai Temple.

There are, however, gifted and skilled individuals striving to reach their true goals and actualize their fullest talents in India who often do not have the means to achieve their true worth. It is a paradox. In this world of extremes, some of the most gifted and talented individuals are considered "lower" members of society due to their caste and are not accepted into academic institutions or job sites merely because they cannot afford the tuition or because they are discriminated against based on their caste. This discrimination resulted in my Bapu's quest for equality in India. Further, imbalanced national policies have prevented India from flowering and achieving universal prosperity. Instead of growing and working together, the caste system causes divisions, creating great civil conflict, increased poverty, malnourishment, and illness lasting centuries. The root of these divisions continue to grow and can be found in the misinterpretation of religious scriptures, human error as well as the seeds sown during Indian colonization.

According to Robert D. Kaplan in his article, "The Coming Anarchy," "to understand the events of the next fifty years, then, one must understand environmental scarcity, cultural and racial clash, geographic destiny, and the transformation of war" (1994). He describes the causes of human conflict and poverty as the result of resource depletion, climate change, ethnic discord and increased intra-state warfare. Thus, as environmental destruction and populations increase simultaneously, the natural result is increased civil tensions and strife. I question the author's logic, however, as he has not fully considered that human growth has also birthed rapid technological advancements, renewable energies and increased social awareness in improving climate change statistics and decreasing poverty rates. These technological advances in communication and engineering are the precise tools we can utilize to commit to sustainable development, green technology and universal education. For instance, Brazil is now the leading producer of sugar-cane based ethanol. This industry has vastly improved Brazil's economy making it one of the four BRIC countries along with Russia, India and China.

In this book I would like to ask the following three analytical questions: How can we, as a global society, prevent the potential of global anarchy in the future as described by Robert D. Kaplan? What has caused the levels of poverty and environmental destruction to reach almost irreversible heights? Do we not see the value and incalculable worth of the natural realm—once lost, irreplaceable?

A compilation of poetry, prose and literary research on development based in India and Uganda, this book shares insights on the development of underprivileged regions of our world in a way that empowers nature along with human inhabitants of the land to insure long term environmental health. In order to answer these three key questions, I would like to share insights from my graduate field work, academic research and statistical data analysis while pursuing an MA in the field of Human Security and Peace building at Royal Roads University.

The poetry stands as a pause or moment of reflection and fresh air between the factual prose. It focuses on two major themes: *human equality* and the *enhancement of human security* through ecological conservation and renewable energy. These two themes are intertwined through a study of ecological biodiversity and environmental harmony.

Through a study of the natural functions of nature—its essence, one becomes aware of the highest level of human functionality—interdependence and harmonious co-existence without harming the vessel of sustenance—our Earth. Nature serves as our daily guide, pointing in a subtle manner towards the power of symbiosis. Symbiotic relationships in nature can help us form the foundation of healthy human networks within the world.

These networks may exist and thrive in a creative fashion without depleting vital natural resources. In essence, nature exists, without permanently impacting any earthly form. So should humans exist and exit the Earth—as a substitute teacher works in a classroom—leaving it as it was found. We should minimize our impact on Earth—it is inherently perfect. A gift to be cherished and adored, honored and loved.

Scribing nature's verse, this work seeks to juxtapose the natural realm with the human world in order to relate the gentle power of the natural world to communicate Truth and a way for humans to walk symbiotically with nature **not against it**. Further, humans are asked to rise above the shallow divisions created by perceived differences and outward appearances (such as colour, caste and the other features of the outer form) and embrace the unity and similarities shared by all humanity—the inner light— as it is embraced by nature. Sharing a common oneness with all humanity—**we may begin to understand the importance of preserving the biochemical structure of nature (functioning as the system of arteries, veins and capillaries within humans).**

We must sustain nature for the future generations of all living organisms—not only humans. Chopping down thousands of acres of ancient forests, spilling billions of gallons of poisonous oil into our oceans, polluting the sky with cars, airplanes, trains and ships, damaging the Earth with thousands of crater-like mines, and building unsustainable housing has depleted the Earth of vital natural resources. It is important to note that instead of contributing to educational and environmental expenditure, many states are also increasing national defence budgets to create nuclear weapons and missiles that are NOT needed and that WILL further pollute the environment, destroy living organisms and create greater unrest and insecurity. Who are we afraid of? Who are we defending ourselves from? It is apparent, that the greatest threat to human and ecological health and welfare is us. ***We are creating ammunition to destroy***

ourselves. Why? As noted in the book, *Leashing the Dogs of War*, the 21st century has witnessed a shift in conflict from inter-state to intra-state warfare. Thus, there is currently less threat of violence beyond state borders. Causes of internal state war and civil conflict include poverty, resource scarcity, gender disparities and racial tensions. To dissipate such conflict, solutions may include increasing national budgets on schooling, health care, agriculture, water transport and regulation, and energy access rather than nuclear weaponry.

According to international statistics, China recently increased its defence budget by 1.5 billion USD in order to protect itself from "potential" threats from surrounding countries in Asia. This in turn has caused the surrounding nations to increase their defence budgets. If one nation was to decrease its defence budget and instead increase federal spending on education and natural rejuvenation policies, new trends and paradigms would be created—fostering peace, education, and environmental sustenance rather than a climate of war and suspicion.

I believe that it is our responsibility as the life forms with advanced neurological functionality, to maintain the health of nature and peace between states. Currently, we are damaging the limbs and arterial systems of Earth and poisoning its waters to a point that its existence is undeniably in danger. The time is now, to prioritize investments in technology rebuilding ecological communities, educational programs and organic agricultural practices rather than creating nuclear weapons. We need a way to develop methods to sustain the natural realm. It is time for humanity to unite and fight for the cause of environmental protection and enhancement as well as human protection—eliminating all nuclear activity and weaponry. If we do not invest in nature today—we will lose our precious Mother Earth who has helped raised us all.

This book is meant to inspire humanity to live as one unit, functioning in a highly efficient and cohesive manner, ensuring the livelihood and well-being of all its members and its sustaining force—mother nature. Nature is our greatest teacher on Earth. Through its subtle and gentle existence, it not only feeds us but it also teaches us about the paths to peace, prosperity and the importance of working cooperatively, without divisions. This construction of nature will help us feed all human communities, reduce poverty and increase quality of life—giving rise to, as Eckharte Tolle so vividly and articulately described in his book, *A New Earth*.

Chapter 1

Improving GDP Per Capita

In terms of socio-political and human development, there are a multitude of possibilities and ways to carve a new path and a new beginning for India and the World. Where multiple castes or socio-economic layers are replaced by one human caste or economic strata giving rise to equality and fundamental human rights and freedoms—the guiding principles held by the most successful states in the 21st century. Not through communism, but through the beauty of a democratic socialism as present in Canada and parts of Europe.

Why is this important? Because more than 37.4% of Indians currently live below the poverty line (Please see Table below). The inability of so many people to achieve their true potential is tragic and is an impediment caused by the lack of support available for students and young adults to find suitable careers and pursue further education or vocational studies. These statistics *can* and *will* be changed through a national system of economic and educational support providing student loans and job placement assistance or employment insurance for graduates.

China, is a country with approximately 157, 033, 277 more people on its soil than India and a comparable GDP. Yet, it has a 2.8% poverty rate within its borders, 34.6% less than the poverty rate currently found in India. What is China doing differently than other nations, creating a lower percentage of poverty among its population? Firstly, Its national policy advocates for the education of all Chinese citizens. China invests a large proportion of its GDP on educational expenditures, hiring foreign teachers with competitive wages in both private and public schools and building international schools with excellent academic standing. In addition, China has invested in a highly efficient national energy production system including renewable energy generated from solar power and hydro power dams extending to all citizens.

In India today, characteristics associated with being lower caste include, high levels of poverty, under-representation in government, and child labour contributing to health insecurity. The health security of low-income families, particularly children can be improved upon the Indian Sub-continent through the implementation of human rights and freedoms, universal health care strategies as well as sustainable development. In order to develop sustainable strategies, I have investigated the harmful physical and psychological health risks associated with slum life such as, contaminated food and drinking water, malnutrition, unsanitary living conditions and abuse. Further, I have explored how renewable energy technologies can help to mitigate the growing poverty rate and enhance per capita income in underprivileged communities by providing reliable electricity to all areas.

USD 2009	GDP	GDP per capita	Inflation Rate	Unemploy-ment Rate	External Debt	Population	Poverty Rate
India (5)	$3,560,000,000,000	$3,100	10.9%	10.7%	223,900,000,000	1,173,108,018 0-14yrs.: 165,285,592	37.4% (Tendkur Report)
USA (2)	$14,260,000,000,000	$46,400	-0.30%	9.3%	13,450,000,000,000	310,232,863	12%
China (3)	$8,789,000,000,000	$6,600	0.7%	4.3%	347,100,000,000	1,330,141,295	2.8%
Japan (4)	$4,137,000,000,000	$32,600	-1.40%	5.10%	2,132,000,000,000	126,804,433	NA%
Italy (11)	$1,760,000,000,000	$30,300	0.80%	7.7%		58,126,212	NA%

Sustainable development through the power of the natural elements such as, electrical expansion through renewable energy, and natural bio-fuels (from sugar cane, corn and jatrofa plants harvested in waste land and desert areas) will help provide the energy needs to produce crops, light homes, provide drinking water, cooling systems and increase income generation. Renewable energy is an important way to bridge divides between social classes. With a greater national investment in renewable technologies for households, communities, cities and states to achieve energy access, underprivileged populations within India and the world can compete in the work force and enjoy an enhanced standard of living at lower long term costs with less impact on the environment. It is through the power of the natural elements that true equality and lasting harmony can prevail among the human race.

I recently participated in an internship in India, where I conducted research on extending energy access through solar energy to underprivileged households and shantytowns. There are barriers to energy access preventing over **two hundred million** households from achieving consistent electrical access in rural areas. Energy access helps enhance the quality of life as it provides increased employment opportunities, food security and academic opportunities reducing poverty levels and conflict (as noted by Ayer). A shift to greener technologies is a way to promote equality and reduce poverty in India and the world.

Further, poverty and violent conflict can be prevented through equal resource distribution and the promotion of human rights. This can be achieved through equal access to green, renewable energy. In India, for instance, there is an abundance of solar energy penetrating the earth in most states that can provide for the lighting, cooling and water heating needs of the entire sub-continent. Hydro power, solar, wind power and other sources of renewable energy have the vast potential of lifting millions of individuals out of poverty.

Chapter 2

Universal Rights and Freedoms of Living

We are One

Each particle of existence
    Every drop of water
All grains of sand
    Every blade of grass
The last spark of fire
    Every buried bone
Every animal spirit
    Every ray of sun
Each drop of moonlight
    Every luminous star
Every galaxy, near, afar
    Is one part—one spoke
On the wheel of life.
    Carrying the universal chariot.
A united force that
    Creates, moves, exists
In cohesive unity
    contributes
To the harmony of all that is
    Moving in time.
If one spoke of the wheel
    Breaks, its entirety,
Its essence is threatened.

The absence of adequate energy access and education has led to increased poverty rates for millions of Daliths. There are approximately 200-250 million Daliths living in India and 75-80% of them live below the poverty line without access to adequate health care, food or shelter (Grey, 2005). As such, health security among the Dalith population is much lower than members of other social classes within India. Recent studies indicate that Daliths are more frequently diagnosed with TB, HIV, anaemia, and blindness than the broader Indian population (Grey, 2005). Further, Dalith women are undernourished, endure pregnancy and post-pregnancy complications, increased maternal mortality and often face domestic violence and abuse. Of the total population, 76.4% of Dalith women are illiterate, reducing their ability to enter the Indian economy (Grey, 2005). Their children are often born with a low birth weight increasing risks of infant mortality (43% of children in India under the age of 5 years are malnourished). Over 50 million underprivileged children in India are orphaned, neglected or sold to work for a lifetime as bonded labourers . . . otherwise known as slaves. The majority of whom have very few opportunities to enrol in schools providing a quality education and obtaining high ranking jobs because of their ancestry. In India today, there are 25,000 landless peasants who have been promised territory by the government but who are yet to receive it (2009). Four key reasons have contributed to widespread suffering, displacement and high disease rates among Daliths:

a.) The majority of the Dalith population in India lives below the poverty line (BPL) and are forced to work in menial and often hazardous labour conditions. The international BPL stands at $1.25USD a day whereas the Indian BPL is $1.08 USD a day, excluding a vast number of individuals and families who may require state assistance.

b.) Daliths are under-represented in the democratic government of India.

c.) Dalith children are less likely to attend primary and secondary school.

d.) Daliths often do not have access to adequate health care.

Living below the poverty line, a large percentage of Daliths inhabit slums, shanty towns, migrant communities (residing in mobile makeshift homes), or government-neglected rural areas. Although the Indian government projects minority representation in public and private sectors, Daliths are often inactive in government decision making.

The Canadian Charter of Human Rights and Freedoms has brought liberation and prosperity to Canada for over a century. I believe that this type of Charter written and implemented in India can have an equal impact:

Canadian Charter of Rights and Freedoms

PART I OF THE CONSTITUTION ACT March 29th, 1982
PART I
CANADIAN CHARTER OF RIGHTS AND FREEDOMS
Whereas Canada is founded upon principles that recognize the supremacy of God and the rule of law:
Guarantee of Rights and Freedoms
Rights and freedoms in Canada

1. The *Canadian Charter of Rights and Freedoms* guarantees the rights and freedoms set out in it subject only to such reasonable limits prescribed by law as can be demonstrably justified in a free and democratic society.

Fundamental Freedoms

2. Everyone has the following fundamental freedoms:

(a) freedom of conscience and religion;

(b) freedom of thought, belief, opinion and expression, including freedom of the press and other media of communication;

(c) freedom of peaceful assembly; and

(d) freedom of association.

Democratic Rights

Democratic rights of citizens

3. Every citizen of Canada has the right to vote in an election of members of the House of Commons or of a legislative assembly and to be qualified for membership therein.

Maximum duration of legislative bodies

4. (1) No House of Commons and no legislative assembly shall continue for longer than five years from the date fixed for the return of the writs of a general election of its members.[81]

Continuation in special circumstances

(2) In time of real or apprehended war, invasion or insurrection, a House of Commons may be continued by Parliament and a legislative assembly may be

continued by the legislature beyond five years if such continuation is not opposed by the votes of more than one-third of the members of the House of Commons or the legislative assembly, as the case may be.

Annual sitting of legislative bodies
5. There shall be a sitting of Parliament and of each legislature at least once every twelve months.

Mobility Rights
Mobility of citizens
6. (1) Every citizen of Canada has the right to enter, remain in and leave Canada.

Rights to move and gain livelihood
(2) Every citizen of Canada and every person who has the status of a permanent resident of Canada has the right
(a) to move to and take up residence in any province; and
(b) to pursue the gaining of a livelihood in any province.

Limitation
(3) The rights specified in subsection (2) are subject to
(a) any laws or practices of general application in force in a province other than those that discriminate among persons primarily on the basis of province of present or previous residence; and
(b) any laws providing for reasonable residency requirements as a qualification for the receipt of publicly provided social services.

Affirmative action programs

(4) Subsections (2) and (3) do not preclude any law, program or activity that has as its object the amelioration in a province of conditions of individuals in that province who are socially or economically disadvantaged if the rate of employment in that province is below the rate of employment in Canada.

Legal Rights

Life, liberty and security of person

7. Everyone has the right to life, liberty and security of the person and the right not to be deprived thereof except in accordance with the principles of fundamental justice.

Search or seizure

8. Everyone has the right to be secure against unreasonable search or seizure.

Detention or imprisonment

9. Everyone has the right not to be arbitrarily detained or imprisoned.

Arrest or detention

10. Everyone has the right on arrest or detention

(a) to be informed promptly of the reasons therefore;

(b) to retain and instruct counsel without delay and to be informed of that right; and

(c) to have the validity of the detention determined by way of *habeas corpus* and to be released if the detention is not lawful.

Proceedings in criminal and penal matters

11. Any person charged with an offence has the right

(a) to be informed without unreasonable delay of the specific offence;

(b) to be tried within a reasonable time;

(c) not to be compelled to be a witness in proceedings against that person in respect of the offence;

(d) to be presumed innocent until proven guilty according to law in a fair and public hearing by an independent and impartial tribunal;

(e) not to be denied reasonable bail without just cause;

(f) except in the case of an offence under military law tried before a military tribunal, to the benefit of trial by jury where the maximum punishment for the offence is imprisonment for five years or a more severe punishment;

(g) not to be found guilty on account of any act or omission unless, at the time of the act or omission, it constituted an offence under Canadian or international law or was criminal according to the general principles of law recognized by the community of nations;

(h) if finally acquitted of the offence, not to be tried for it again and, if finally found guilty and punished for the offence, not to be tried or punished for it again; and

(i) if found guilty of the offence and if the punishment for the offence has been varied between the time of commission and the time of sentencing, to the benefit of the lesser punishment.

12. Everyone has the right not to be subjected to any cruel and unusual treatment or

13. A witness who testifies in any proceedings has the right not to have any incriminating evidence so given used to incriminate that witness in any other proceedings, except in a prosecution for perjury or for the giving of contradictory evidence.

Interpreter

14. A party or witness in any proceedings who does not understand or speak the language in which the proceedings are conducted or who is deaf has the right to the assistance of an interpreter.

Equality Rights

Equality before and under law and equal protection and benefit of law

15. (1) Every individual is equal before and under the law and has the right to the equal protection and equal benefit of the law without discrimination and, in particular, without discrimination based on race, national or ethnic origin, colour, religion, sex, age . . . (Canadian Charter, 1982)[1]

---

[1]   Canadian Charter of Rights and Freedoms. Retrieved on August 25, 2011 from http://laws-lois.justice.gc.ca/eng/Const/page-15.html. Department of Justice Canada.

Chapter 3

Origins of the Caste System and its Manifestations

Atomic Dance

With perfect elegance and grace
 They dance in unison
  Not a step out of place
   Upon the grand cosmos

 The stage of the universe
 Unending it grows
In constant harmony
  Creating new tunes

   The unseen spheres
    Which dance within us all
     Make up all that is
      Grace every pristine place

    Waltzing in eternal bliss
    Atoms bloom within
    Every Sunkist petal
   Extend every flowering branch

Soar through every oceanic
Crest, every rising wave
   Compose every grain of sand
    Every sparkling ray

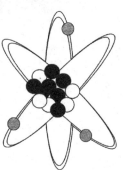

    It is true
      The atomic dance composed within me
     Is composed too
    Within every utter entity
   As it is within you

Self knowledge and Enlightenment

What is Brahman? "It is the supreme indestructible living entity; the material nature of which is called the self."—*Adhyatma*

Being a Brahman (currently considered the highest Hindu caste in India) is not a caste, it is a way of life. In the Sacred Bhagavad Gita, it is stated:

> "Those who strive for liberation from old age and death take refuge in Me and are Brahman, because they understand transcendental activity."

Those people who "act piously in this life are liberated from the delusions of dualities and serve me with determination and faith."

- *Adhibhuta*—physical nature, constantly changing
- *Adhivadaiva*—universal form of the Lord, demigods, Sun, moon
- *Adhi-yajna*—supersoul situated in all living entities

As stated in Sri Bhagavad Gita:

> "All who take refuge in Me, even the low born, women, merchants, as well as the working class, attain the supreme goal" (Bhagavad Gita, p. 543).

In the Bhagavad Gita, Prince Arjuna (a sacred warrior and archer in the Mahabharata) said to God:

"You are the Supreme Brahman, the Supreme abode, and the Supreme purifier. You are the eternal divine person, the Primal God, unborn and omnipresent" (p. 561).

Are Brahmans greater than God who lives in the hearts of all?

In the Sri Bhagavad Gita, Lord Krishna describes Himself-

"I am the Self, O Gudakesa, abiding in the hearts of all beings. I am the beginning, the middle, and the end of all beings" (p. 571). "God is the seed of all existence" (p. 591).

As such, all people are the created equal. If we disrespect and de-value people, is that not likened to disrespecting the God in all people? To classify and subordinate a part of the world, a part of God, a part of the creation, and souls, as untouchable is a great guna or sin. If we believe that the creation is ultimately Divine and created by God and a part of God, then is it not important to respect and worship every part of the creation? Humans are an important part of the world and the universe, thus they should be treated with dignity and respect as all living species on Earth and not divided based on superficial and unfounded principles and immeasurable qualities.

Caste in the Shadows

The Caste system is intricately ingrained into every aspect of Indian society as it has been for thousands of years. Although the constitution and predominant religions in India do not acknowledge the caste system as an appropriate mode of human organization, Indian culture has interpreted religion to suit the constructs of a hierarchical system of human classification. Many individuals such as Dr. Ambedkar and Mahatma Gandhi, and Sikh teachers such as Guru Nanak Dev Ji, have protested against such inequality and discrimination. Advocacy groups and numerous civil society organizations such as SPARC (Society for the Protection of Area Resource Centres), Peace-Child India, and Arivu, attempt to promote the rights of Daliths. Unfortunately, most efforts to eradicate the caste system are only minimally successful. Hence, the number people living in slums, shanty towns, migrant communities, and on the streets multiply each year.

Origins of the caste system

Although the caste system was once a "social system … harmoniously aligning different talents in society . . . over time this well-functioning system was corrupted by a [desire] for power and prestige" (Rai, 2008, p.164). Following its disintegration, the social divides in the caste system led to the creation of a class which primarily engaged in street work, cleaning excrement and filth. They were named the Untouchables as the "upper" classes did not want to become "polluted" by interacting with them (Rai, 2008, p. 164). Despite its illegality in India, I assert that the caste system still pervasively degrades the social well-being, economic security, physical and psychological health security, and environmental security of Dalith children and families.

For thousands of years, untouchables or Daliths have remained "at the bottom of the scale- some may say off the scale altogether" (Ninian, 2008, p. 186). Dr. Ambedkar (1892-1956) served as one of the first leaders and advocates of the Daliths, acknowledging the injustice of their treatment. His account was one of the earliest coherent critiques of the paradigm of the "Hindu Right" (Sharma, 2005, p. 843). Dr. Ambedkar notes the historical origins of the caste system as well as the geographical and socio-political aspects and flaws in this hierarchical ideology. He advocated minority protection, majority rule as well as the option of Buddhism for Daliths rather than Hinduism (Sharma, 2005).

Health concerns among Daliths

Following the independence of India, in 1950, the caste system was removed from the constitution and considered an illegal social construct. **Still, conditions have regressed for Daliths.** Slum communities have grown, health insecurity has multiplied, and discrimination has increased due to their inability to enter the professional work field and the private sector and to obtain a high quality education.

Daliths continue to face immense health security risks as well. In terms of nutritional status, for instance, India ranks amongst the lowest in global health and well-being, primarily due to the health conditions of Daliths. According to the UNDP, human development report, 46% of children in India are underweight (UNDP, 2009).

the prevalence of iron deficiency anemia ranges from 13.4% in Thailand to 87% in India . . . The region also has the highest burden of low birth weight infants (ranging from 9% in Thailand to 30% in India) . . . the prevalence of moderate-to-severe stunting ranges from 12% in Thailand to almost 50% in . . . India (WHO, 2008).

A report conducted by the World Economic Forum in 2006, reveals that India has "grossly inadequate performance in health services for her teeming millions, as well as failures in primary education and infrastructure" (Rai, 2008, p. 151).

In India, "the officially outlawed caste system may still dictate one's destiny from birth" (Rai, 2008, p. 6). The caste system is a normal part of everyday life. In these areas, Daliths can only work in jobs involving animal carcasses, leather, night soil, scavenging, toilet cleaning, floor sweeping, street cleaning or bonded labor.

Not only do Daliths face incalculable social inequalities, injustices and health risks but they are also the victims of crime and discrimination. "National statistics in 2005 registered 110,000 cases of crimes against Daliths based on caste. These included violence, abuse and murder . . ." (Ninian, 2008, p. 189). Further, Dalith families often work "on the streets . . . living with no more shelter than a makeshift tent, or, worse, sleeping on the sidewalks and in alleyways with no protection at all" (Rai, 2008, p. 214).

Child Labour as a result of Caste Distinction

According to the International Labour Office there are an estimated 217.7 million children aged 5-14 years who must work for survival around the world at present (ILO, 2006). Despite its illegality, child labour remains a significant problem in many states such as, China, India, Afghanistan, Sub-Saharan Africa and certain Middle Eastern countries.[2] In Sub-Saharan Africa 26.4 percent of children aged 5-14 were "economically active" in 2004 (ILO, 2006, p. 9).

In the same year there were an estimated 190 million child labourers globally of which over one hundred million worked under hazardous conditions. While the incidence of child labour is highest in Sub-Saharan Africa, the *largest number* of child workers is found in the Asia-Pacific region (ILO, 2006, para. 1). It is important to note, however, that the global number of child labourers dropped 11 percent between 2002-2006, while that of children in hazardous work decreased by 26 percent (ILO, 2006, p. 7).

In India, the overall rate of child labour has decreased at the rate of, 0.003% between 1991-2001. Currently, there are roughly 22 million working children out of a total 253 million children in the country, the largest number of child labourers in the world. Child labour takes many forms in India, including that of domestic labour, hazardous industrial work, export industry work, working in sweat shops, and child bonded labour in the agriculture industry (HDR, 2009, p. 2)[3]

---

[2]   See Appendices #2 and 3
[3]   See Appendix #4

The lower caste children (under fourteen) often illegally engage in hazardous and high-risk work such as child bonded labour impacting their health and well-being. This may include working long hours with no job security or stability in sharecropping, casual wage labour, mining, brick making, rice mills, carpet weaving, match factories, stone cutting and quarries (ILO, 2009, p. 4). They may be laid off without notice, impacting the family income.

Social inequities such as the lack of social services, employment insurance, health care, sound public education, and pervasive application of a deeply-embedded caste system (classifying some as "untouchable" and therefore unemployable), high poverty rates and child marriages often lead to increased child labour. For instance, a family that cannot afford to send a child to school often decides to have the child contribute to domestic labour at home or to begin work to supplement the family income. Thus, the lack of available and affordable public education programs for children often prevent children from lower socio-economic backgrounds from pursuing a basic education or vocational studies.

It was found in a study conducted by Saswati Das and Diganta Mukherjee, for instance, that a child's level of education impacts their probability of becoming a child labourer. They took a study of over 1200 children analysing four levels of education. In one of their study's of over 600 children it was found that 41.84% of male child labourers and 43.69% of female child labourers had no education. Additionally, they discovered that 27.82% of male child labourers and 25.23% of female child labourers only had obtained a level one education. There were 22.76% of males and 22.52% of females with a level two education. Further, there were only 7.59% of surveyed male child labourers and only 8.56% of surveyed female child labourers with a level three education (Das & Mukherjee, 2008, p. 314). This study underscores the common-sense conclusion that children with higher levels of education are less likely to become child labourers.

Education and the Caste System

To a large extent, class structures determine the future of many children in India. If they do not have an education or vocational training, many children pursue familial lines of work based on family tradition, rather than on personal ambition or talent. As expressed by Vinay Rai, "the officially outlawed caste system may still dictate one's destiny from birth" (Rai, 2007, p. 6). Many lower caste children in South Asian countries are engaged in child bonded labour. This may include work in sharecropping, casual wage labour, mining, brick making, rice mills, carpet weaving, sexual exploitation, match factories, stone cutting and quarries (ILO, 2009, p. 4). Poverty stricken families who are in debt or loan-bound may be forced to involve their children in free labour to pay off their debts—furthering them into economic dependence and non-progression. According to a report concerning child labour in Asia conducted by the ILO, "forced labour, primarily in the form of debt bondage, is found amongst low castes, minorities, and migrants, who suffer additionally from discrimination and social exclusion" (ILO, 2009, p. 4). In addition to the current world economic system, social imbalances within states, such as imbalanced class structures, gender inequalities, underdeveloped labour laws, an absence of labour unions, disregard for constitutional laws, and high rates of poverty and disease have contributed to the degradation of working conditions, unmonitored migrant work and employment of child labourers impacting their community security, food security, economic security, environmental security and social security. Using the construction industry as an example, children may help to build apartments, homes or government structures which can take anywhere from several months to many years to complete. They work long hours and receive little pay, typically earning only enough to provide the bare necessities to their families.

During my work at Peace Child International, I interned for over five months with a migrant community in Bangalore. We taught literacy and nutritional skills to some of the migrant children in an informal setting. Although there were many teenagers in the migrant community, we had very few kids over the age of thirteen in our class. Migrating throughout the year in search of work on construction sites, children (as young as eight or nine) of migrant workers in India are often expected to work alongside their parents. They often assist their parents with shovelling, transporting materials and cleaning. In addition, underage children are often left to handle the household while their parents are working. This includes cooking, cleaning, getting water from the local water source, and raising their younger siblings. If they are not at the job site, children as young as six or seven are expected to maintain the household and raise younger siblings while parents are working. Due to lack of time, economic instability and constant travel, children of migrant workers are unable to enrol in consistent educational programs or to pursue vocational studies. Hence, the cycle continues.

Underprivileged children, if abandoned or orphaned, are often sent to underfunded public children's homes under state custody. The Karnataka State Children's Home is one example. It is a multi-functional institution, serving as a shelter for children who have been abused or neglected, runaway, abandoned, orphaned or who are mentally or physically challenged. If the children are not claimed or do not enrol in the boarding school, they remain in the shelter well into adulthood. The Home houses over five hundred children, many of whom attempt to escape. The children here are often neglected by the house mothers and fathers and often contract diseases such as, tuberculosis and hepatitis due to hazardous living conditions. Because of the high turnover rate of teachers in the Children's Home, there is no consistent learning program. The children (aged five to nineteen) are often beaten by peers and care takers, eat un-nutritious food, sleep and live in unsanitary quarters.

To a large extent, class structures determine the future of many children in India as many of them do not have an education or opportunities for vocational training. In one district consisting of 700 Dalith families, only three children went to school. Instead, as noted above, they begin work before the age of fourteen. Currently, there are approximately 20 million working children in India (most of them Daliths) out of a total 253 million children in the country (Grey, 2005).

The Need for Change

According to the United Nations (UN), in both developing and industrial countries, threats to health security are usually greater for poor people in rural areas, particularly children. Increased health risks are often associated with malnutrition, insufficient medical supplies and facilities, clean water or other necessities for healthcare (UNDP, 1994). According to Vinay Rai, "twenty-two percent of the world's poor live in India, battling hunger and disease (Rai, p. 212)." This figure is supported by the State of the World's Children report conducted by the World Health Organization (2008), noting that only half of the Indian population receives appropriate antenatal and neonatal care—the lack of which is the central cause of infant mortality world wide (WHO, 2008). Without regular access to health care or resources, Daliths are less likely to receive appropriate health care for pregnant mothers and newborn children (SPARC, 2004-05).

Although one part of India is growing rapidly in software infrastructure and technological advancements, the other part of India "trudges on, still lacking clean drinking water, enough food, basic education, decent health care, and wholesome housing" (Rai, 2007, p. 212). Reducing the extent of poverty in these areas may help improve the health security among Daliths. Research in the area of disease rates among Dalith families, particularly blindness as well as governmental and non-governmental initiatives aimed at improving their livelihood may greatly enhance living conditions.

Development Strategies

The Society for the Promotion of Area Resource Centers (SPARC) is one of the largest NGOs in Asia. It operates from Mumbai and supports two civil society movements: the National Slum Dwellers Federation (NSDF) and Mahila

Milan (women together). SPARC assists hundreds of thousands of slum dwellers and pavement dwellers learn about affordable housing, savings, credit, building and toilet construction, housing exhibitions, enumeration, rehabilitation and dialogue with government bodies. SPARC maintains that "in the absence of planned housing for the poor, communities make do with whatever material they can find and they locate their dwellings wherever they can" (SPARC, 2004-05, p. 4). SPARC receives funding from a multitude of foreign investors such as, the International Institute for Environment and Development, the Water and Sanitation Program of the World Bank and the Swedish International Development Agency (SIDA). It also receives funding from the Indian Micro Credit Fund and Revolving Funds to achieve project goals (SPARC, 2004).

In terms of labour development, India is currently developing its eleventh Five Year Plan (2007-2012) in the area of labour development. The focus of the plan will be unemployment, underemployment, regular wage in the work force and addressing the needs of employees in the unstructured sectors of society such as, manual labour (B. Joseph et al., 2009, p. 226). Further, the government of India has exponentially increased its budget (144%) for the NREGA Bharat Nirman program that seeks to improve infrastructure in rural villages (New Delhi, Link, 2009).

Ambavaram Village

We have started a sustainable development project in Ambavaram Village, Andhra Pradesh through coordination between the Society for Deprived Classes Education and the Lotus Foundation for Children (LFC). The project has helped provide solar lighting in the village school and Church as well as a solar lamp post, water pump, water tank, compost and Jatrofa plantation. We now plan to build an eco-friendly kindergarten, primary school and vocational school for the Dalith community in Ambavaram.

Chapter 4

Efficient Use of Renewable Energy to Achieve Economic Stabilization

Breathing Sun

How can I describe the sun
Which enlightens my earthly eye
Everyday through rain and cloud
Theheart of the pale blue sky

It beats in steady pulse
Searing veins of flowing light
Through the hungry Earth
Feeding every thirsty life

As the setting sun calms its pulsing waves
Its blood red image
Streaks our darkening plain
Weaving an intricate web

With all colours of the spectrum
It composes its glorious scene
Blending all hues reflected on the sea
Upon the blushing sky—all hues into one

Even through our nightly sleep
The warming sun
Beats unstopped
Feeding every sprouting seed

Energy is at the heart of most critical economic, environmental and developmental issues facing the world today ... Current energy systems are inadequate to meet the needs of the world's poor and are jeopardizing the achievement of the Millennium Development Goals (MDGs) ... in the absence of reliable energy services, neither health clinics nor schools can function properly.[4]

Energy is an essential building block of human life. It powers the light in our homes, heat on our floors and the fuel in our cars. Energy has shaped and moulded our human world in a profound way. We rely on electricity, for instance, to expand communities in terms of agriculture, industrial production, education, and health care—"Development and electrification are mutually reinforcing" (Pan & Peng, 2006, p. 83). Unfortunately, in terms of environmental consequences, our high levels of energy consumption have been powered by conventional and often polluting agents such as, coal, gas and fossil fuels. These harmful agents have compromised planetary preservation, causing ecological shifts and atmospheric changes—in turn, threatening human well-being. Further, most Dalith abodes do not have *any* source of electricity or water generation.

Over consumption of coal, fossil fuels and gases for land and water transportation and other devices have caused a build up of carbon dioxide in our atmosphere. Now, not only are fossil fuels drastically shifting ice patterns in the Arctic, they are causing the entire planet to warm due to increased oceanic temperatures. In the 20th century the average world temperature increased by 0.6

---

[4]   *Energy for a Sustainable Future.* The Secretary General's Advisory Group on Energy and Climate Change: Summary Report and Recommendations (2010). United Nations.

degrees Celsius which is enough to cause many challenges. Recently, part of the inter-continental ice shelf over the Barents Sea collapsed. Further ice shifts are seen in the Arctic peninsula. Climate change also directly challenges the lives of Northern Indigenous groups and Arctic animal species reliant on the thick sea ice to hunt seals. **In contemplating energy expansion, it is important to note the devastating impacts current forms of energy have on our planet and its diverse species everyday (AGECC, 2010).**

Despite the impacts of conventional sources of power and electricity, energy is required to maintain healthy standards of living. The goal is to achieve global energy access to decrease poverty levels without further negative impacts on environmental health. An astonishingly large proportion of earth's population currently does not have basic energy access. Approximately 34% of the world's population or 2.4 billion people in remote rural areas of developing countries do not have any access to consistent and reliable electrical supply. For instance, only 25% of households in Africa have access to electricity (World Bank, 2011). In India, almost half the population has little or no power supply (IEA, 2010) the majority of whom are Daliths. Although developing nations have experienced significant economic development in the past decade through industrial sector growth such as, information technology, foreign trade and investment, finance, national security, science and innovation they still face significant voids in electrical supply. India, for instance, now has the fifth largest economy in the world behind only the US, China, Japan and the European Union. Indeed, it serves an important role in international decision-making bodies such as, the G20 Group of Nations. In terms of social growth and human development, however, one third or 37% of India's population of one billion exist below the poverty line (UNDP, 2010) (Please see Appendix 1). Approximately 42% of the Indian population lives on $1.25 a day and 55% lives in a state of multi-dimensional poverty (MPI) (UNDP, 2010). India's Human Development Index is 119 out of the world's 169 nations (UNDP, 2011) (Please see Appendix 2).

Yet, India and parts of Sub-Saharan Africa have the opportunity today, to choose alternative sources of energy. As technology in the field of renewable energy grows, it offers a multitude of energy options for developing countries to invest in their natural resources, promoting ecological growth and human well being. Developing countries have the opportunity to conserve their pristine landscapes by avoiding overconsumption of fossil fuels. They can become leaders in green energy technologies for lighting, heating and transportation needs promoting both human security and bio-diversity.

The Importance of Energy Access

Energy access as described in this document operates on three levels of daily human functioning, based on the UN Summary Report on Energy and Climate Change. Level one: Electricity, fossil fuels, technologies for lighting, cooking, heating, health, education, and community services. Level two: Electricity and modern fuels for energy services for increased production. Level three: Modern energy services for advanced in home/office heating, cooling systems for space and water as well as personal vehicle transportation.

Architect Suhasini Ayer, living in Auroville, Tamil Nadu writes about the difficulties related to living without electricity even for a few days following a cyclone:

Jan. 1, 2012

01st Jan 2012; as it started for us in Auroville . . . .

The movie "2012" was released in 2010 in anticipation of the year that started today; the makers of this Hollywood drama were building on the predictions of the Mayan calendar which supposedly ends the world as we know it on 21st Dec 2012. Watching John Cusack race down a road that kept unravelling behind him or run up the hill with monster waves catching his heels, I decided that I will stay off the roads and stick to the hills when this year starts.

Christmas morning, instead of going to church to give thanks for the birth of our saviour, I was catching the BBC show on the worst weather phenomena of the year 2011, ended by a lady smirking into the camera saying "2011 will be the worst year since beginning of time in terms of weather related disasters globally". Obviously we did not watch the same movies!

With just couple of days left for "worst weather year" to wind down, a depression that had been aimlessly hanging around in the Bay of Bengal decided to drop in. For some reason the beach landing at Pondicherry angered it mightily; turning it into a banshee with a mean and viscous temper. The cyclonic winds howled and gusted through the night and most of the next day tearing up the trees and buildings, snapping the electrical cables and poles accompanied with rain that was more like water cannons at work!

When the show wound up, we found ourselves with the task of clearing thousands of downed trees, hacking through blocked roads and working the bureaucracy of the state electrical board. Life as we know it seems to be underpinned on electrical energy. Live without it for 2 days and everything unravels. You cannot work, meet deadlines, shop / store or feed yourself, attend to personal hygiene and for communication you have to make conversation in real time.

A few days following the cyclone in Auroville, Suhasini found herself providing water to over 12,000 people. Her email reads:

Jan. 5, 2012

Dear Pavan,
I am bit overwhelmed after the cyclone as I have taken up the work of trying to coordinate between the state electricity board to get the energy infrastructure up and going again while trying to organize on a daily basis drinking water supply to 3 villages (12,000 people). So I am in the office only intermittently as I keep getting distress calls from the field. I think after the 10th Jan'12 I will be back to work.

Suhasini

Three key global strategies have been adopted by various nations to expand electricity to rural and remote areas. These include: Grid extension, mini-grid systems, and off-grid decentralized energy access (UN, 2010).

Energy access as described in this document operates on three levels of daily human functioning, based on the UN Summary Report on Energy and Climate Change:

Level one: Electricity, fossil fuels, and technologies for lighting, cooking, heating, health,
education, and community services.
- Electricity: 50-100kWh/person each year
- Biomass cook stove: 50-100 kgoe of fuel or biomass/year

Level two: Electricity and modern fuels for energy services for increased production.
- Irrigation: water pump mechanisms
- Fertilizer: mechanical cultivation and land tilling
- Transport fuel: tractors and goods or produce vehicles
- Agricultural process (i.e. cheese production)

Level three: Modern energy services for advanced in home/office heating and cooling systems for space and water as well as personal vehicle transportation.
- Electricity: 2000kWh/person each year

There are three key strategies adopted by various nations to expand electricity to rural and remote areas. These include:
- Grid extension
- Mini-grid systems
- Off-grid decentralized energy access (UN, 2010)

Mini grid energy access involves linking a community or village to a small-scale decentralized grid which generates enough power to provide electricity for that particular block. This small low-voltage grid may be connected to a number of smaller power generating sources including hydro power, wind turbines and other conventional and non-conventional energy sources. Mini-grid systems have been widely utilized in China, Tunisia, Mali and Sri Lanka. Renewable energies such as, bio-energy, wind, small hydro and solar power are best suited for off-grid and mini grid energy systems. Off-grid, decentralized energy access is electricity supply to one point of need such as, a home, school, clinic or Church. The main challenges for off-grid systems include increased investment costs, maintenance of the systems and accurate pricing (UN, AGECC, 2010).

Requiring the expansion of transmission and distribution of electricity to communities, grid extension was widely used by the Chinese government in the 1990s to expand electricity in rural villages. In the same decade, China provided electricity to thirty villages per day and extended electricity to 700 million households—it now has over 95% electrical capacity (Please see Appendix 2). In South Africa over 2.5 million households were connected to the grid in less than seven years and over 95 percent of households in Vietnam received energy access through grid extension (AGECC, 2010). Grid extension links a community or village to a decentralized grid which generates enough power to provide electricity for that particular block or community. The main challenges for grid extension include increased investment costs, maintenance of the systems and accurate pricing (UN, AGECC, 2010).

Multi-Dimensional Poverty and Inequality

Energy access has significant impacts on poverty levels in a state. Multi-dimensional inequality (MDI) is the extent to which inequality is manifest across dimensions of living including health, education, social status, gender and income level due to the unequal distribution of wealth in a state. According to S. Seth, if the inequality or economic stability of one group rises and the other is unaltered, then overall inequality rises in a society (2009). In India, MDI is found in every state. Partly due to the caste system in which the sub group of Daliths have been confined to a certain economic niche for centuries while other sub groups (higher castes) are steadily expanding across socio-economic dimensions. In South Asia and India, large losses are noted in Health (31%) and Education (41%) due to unequal distribution of wealth and resources (HDR, 2010). As noted in the UNDP Human Development Report: "The dimensions of poverty go far beyond inadequate income—to poor health and nutrition, low education and skills, inadequate livelihoods, bad housing conditions, social exclusion and lack of participation" (HDR, 2010). Multi-dimensional poverty is often more predominant in states with lower levels of energy access. Electrical access in urban centres (89%) is much higher than in rural areas (51%) of India. Over 350,000 rural villages lack sufficient energy access. Orissa, one of the poorest states in India, is one of the three States in India facing the most considerable deficits in energy access. Only 26.9% of the residents in Orissa, 24.3 % of the residents in Jarkhand and 10.7% of the residents in Bihar, had energy access in 2001 (Appendix 3).

Further, 93% of the poverty-stricken individuals in Orissa live in rural areas working as small and marginal farmers or casual wage labourers facing a significant lack of employment opportunities. In many cases, their socio-economic status inhibits them from attaining energy access. Many of the poor in the internal regions of the country depend on forests for their sustenance—they "have limited or no voice in decision making" (UNDP, 2004, p. 5). According to the UN Human Development report on Orissa, the Human Development Index (a measure of State health index, education index and income index) of Orissa is 0.404, when compared with Kerala (o.638) and Bihar (0.367) 11th out of 15 states in India (UN, p. 15, 2004). Human Development Index: 16 out of 30 districts within Orissa have a lower HDI than India's which is 0.519 (UNDP, 2004). And India's HDI is lower than the world HDI of 0.663.

- Top Five Districts in Orissa: *Khurda, Jharsuguda, Cuttack, Sundergarh, Deogarh*
- High need Districts in Orissa: *Malklanagiri, Kandhamal, Gajapati, Koraput, Nabarangpur* (Please see Appendix 4)

Top 5 Orissan Districts with the highest HDI levels:

District Name	Un-Electrified	Electrified
1. Khorda	94	1120
2. Jharsuguda	16	305
3. Cuttack	15	1693
4. Sundargarh	641	883
5. Debagarh	338	317

High Need Orissan Districts with the lowest HDI levels:

District Name	Un-Electrified	Electrified
6. Malklanagiri,	761	156
7. Kandhamal	1416	755
8. Gajapati	633	746
9. Koraput	1262	579
10. Nabarangpur	421	350

The data presented above reveals that the states with a higher percentage of "unelectrified" villages in Orissa tend to have lower levels of human development (Please see Appendix 6).

Renewable Energy Potential in India

In terms of current primary energy supply, India sources its energy from coal, oil, combined renewable and waste, oil, hydro, nuclear, geo-thermal, solar and wind. The largest source of energy is coal (42.1%) and the most insignificant sources of power are geo-thermal, solar and wind (0.2%). It relies heavily on energy from oil (23.3%).

Although not yet fully utilized, India contains significant potential in renewable energies such as, solar, geothermal, and wind energy. In terms of solar energy, it has consistent and regular solar energy penetrating the sub-continent. The deserts of Rajasthan receive abundant light radiation, ranging between 5.8-6.6 KwH/sq. m. Karnataka, Tamil Nadu, Maharashtra, Uttar Pradesh and Gujarat receive between 5.6-6.2 KwH/sq. m. Kerala, Madhya Pradesh, Orissa, Bihar, Punjab, Haryana, Himachal, Goa and West Bengal receive between 5.2-5.8 KwH/sq. m. In the North Eastern states, solar energy ranges from 4.4-5.8 KwH/sq. m. Hydro-power, geo-thermal and wind power are also rich sources of renewable energy in India.

Current Initiatives in the Field of Renewable Energy: Technological Design

As noted above, the solar power potential in India is insurmountable. A minute percentage of the Jasalmer desert in Rajasthan can provide enough solar energy to provide electricity for all Indian households. The same holds true for Africa. Approximately one percent of the Sahara desert in Africa can harness enough solar power to generate electricity for the entire world (TSL, p. 22, 2007). However, there are setbacks to solar energy including, high up front costs and the lack of efficiency in photovoltaic cells. Yet, over time such flaws can be overcome.

Solar photovoltaic energy is a scientific innovation to capture the sun's energy through photovoltaic cells

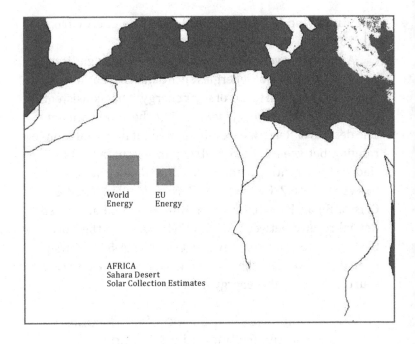

World Energy

EU Energy

AFRICA
Sahara Desert
Solar Collection Estimates

or panels made from silicon and then converted into electricity. The energy is absorbed by solar cells planted on the solar panel which is perched in an area with abundant sunlight. Solar PV electricity can be used to power vehicles, heating and cooling (fans) buildings, swimming pools, indoor water heating, cook stoves and lighting (KREDL, 2010). The solar energy is then transferred by wire through a battery and into a LED or CFL light within a space. The battery for the PV lighting systems lasts about seven to ten years and requires very little maintenance. LED lights are currently more commonly utilized than CFL because of their durability, efficiency and brightness. However, the technological efficiency of photovoltaic cells is presently only 6-12%. The silicon in PV systems contributes to the high up front costs of solar energy production (Das, 2008). There are more cost-effective methods of creating solar cells, however. Nanotechnology, in which solar radiation receptors are made from curved plastic units instead of silicon are highly efficient. Cost-effective technology is used in places such as, Seville, Spain and Pondicherry in Eastern Tamil Nadu, India. Mirror technology for solar energy is an efficient way to capture the sun's energy through a solar dish made from mirrors rather than a solar panel made from PV cells.

The Indian Solar Mission

Solar India is an initiative set out by the government of India to enhance the climate of energy access within India, particularly in rural India where there is a deficiency in electrical capacity in millions of households. Currently, there are 1,326 hamlets and villages without electrical capacity within India (Please see Appendix #6). The Solar India initiative seeks to implement approximately new national policies to catalyze the process of national electrification. Please see Appendix #4. Prospective national policies for "Solar India" include:

1.) Increasing off-grid solar power opportunities—low income households.
2.) Manufacturing capabilities—promoting domestic manufacturing of high end and technologically advanced solar photovoltaic cells and solar power panels.
3.) Research and application of innovative solar power production.

4.) Human Resources—Increased employment of trained personnel in the engineering and management of solar photovoltaic technology.

Appendix 4:
Prospective National Policies for "Solar India"

Recommended Policy	Key Objectives	Strategies for Action
1. Off-grid Solar Power Opportunities—Low Income Households	-utilization of 1000MW of solar power through decentralized methods by 2017	-Ministry of New and Renewable Energy: provide solar lighting for 10,000 households at 90% subsidy through remote village electrification program -Banks to offer low cost credit for grid connected solar lights
2. Manufacturing capabilities	-Domestic manufacturing of low cost highly efficient solar power devices such as, silicon wafers, towards manufacturing concentrating solar collectors and other solar power collectors.	-Special Incentive Package (SIP—elaboration required) towards the local production of low cost manufacturing of silicon and PV plants. -creation of an Incentive Package for the local production of solar thermal technologies. -Financing towards domestic production of solar power through the Indian Renewable Energy Development Agency (IREDA) in the form of small loans (low interest?) and refinancing.
3. Research and Application	-The research and development sector devoted to the Solar India Mission will be involved in researching current, advanced and innovative methods of solar power production and innovations. This division will be involved in testing and researching quality enhancement.	-creation of a Solar Research Council to manage Mission progress and setbacks, need of resources and additional support systems as well as international informational exchange and mutual aid opportunities. -Human resource development and training of 1000 scientists in diverse solar power technologies and energy conversion sites. -Construction of solar power plants with various functions in energy generation.
8. Human Resources	-Employment of 100,000 trained and experienced professionals in solar power by the end of phase 3 (2022) including engineering management development and research -creation of programs to enhance the efficiency of solar power technology through e-programs	-IITs and Engineering Colleges: Development of educational degree programs in Engineering, solar energy and Technology through government subsidies and support -Ministry of Labour to offer a condensed training program to manage skill development for students of solar power servicing and maintenance.

Nodal agencies play a pivotal role in energy development, acting as mediators between the Municipality, the State and the Central governments, connecting a vast network of energy operations.

The Central Government supports a multitude of active and developing policies under the Electricity Act, 2003 to sustain energy operations. The stated aim of the Electricity Act is to consolidate the laws and legal codes related to the management, regulation, development and competition of electrical generation. It aims to implement transparent, accountable and just policies which ensure the universal access and distribution of high quality electrical supply to every district within India. A Tribunal has been established by the Electricity Act to resolve false practices where just and transparent policy implementation has not occurred.

Financing Solar Initiatives

The *global* need for capital investment of basic energy access for all amounts to $25-30 billion dollars per year until 2030. As noted in the AGECC report, accessing and distributing financing will be a challenge. Often, countries invest in infrastructure for commercial and industrial sectors before supplying energy to all inhabitants (2010) as seen widely across India and other developing countries.

One of the objectives of Solar India is to promote entrepreneurship in the field of solar power expansion in order to boost economic capital and investment in solar energy. Financing entrepreneurial projects will be made available through two main avenues: subsidies and soft loans for on or off-grid solar photovoltaic energy. In high need states such as, Orissa, government subsidies may amount to 90% for electrical supply companies and citizens on the initial investment of solar photovoltaic energy. The other form of financing for solar expansion will be soft loans. With the approval of the MNRE, soft loans can be provided at a 5% interest rate from banks and lending institutions such as, REC.

In terms of implementing and achieving deliverables, the Solar India initiative has been divided into three multi-year phases respectively from 2012-2022:

Phase 1 (2012-2013): Grid-based solar power production increased to 1000MW by 2013
- *200MW* decentralized off-grid solar applications in rural areas

Phase 2 (2013-2017): *1000MW* off-grid solar applications
- Scale up grid based solar power production increased to a total of 4000MW by 2017 through mandatory purchase of renewable energy by utilities and preferential tax

Phase 3 (2017-2022): Deployment of 20 million solar lighting systems in rural India
- 2022: solar power to achieve grid parity; distribution of 20,000MW of solar power

Up front, fully loaded costs of solar energy exceed traditional electrical methods. According to the AGECC, the cost of a solar cook stove ranges from $3-12USD per household. The cost of an indoor decentralized solar lighting system (with two LED or CFL lights and a fan) is approximately, $240.00 USD. Thus, a package of a cook stove and indoor lighting would cost about $250.00 USD per household with almost no follow up costs for about a decade of usage. In Indian Rupees, the cost would be around 11,040Rs. for each household, an amount most rural families cannot afford. However, with government subsidization of supplies, affordability may increase. In total there are approximately 359, 485 villages and hamlets which currently do not have electrical capacity in India (Please see Appendix 4).

Applying these costs to 359,485 villages (with an average of 1000 households in each village) shows us that the approximate funding for renewable energies in Indian households will amount to about 2.4% of India's GDP or $86 billion USD. As noted in the Program Guidelines, the project goals and vision for Solar India are exemplary. The commendable goals of the Jawarhalal Nehru Solar Mission (JNNSM), if achieved, will meet the energy needs of the Indian population by 2022 enhancing energy and human security in India.

Chapter 5

The Issues—Barriers to Energy Access in underprivileged Areas

Analyzing two states on extreme ends of the development spectrum in India will help us better understand current needs and focus areas to achieve universal energy access in the state. Orissa is one of the most underdeveloped states in India and Maharashtra is one the most highly urbanized. Orissa has one of the lowest GDSP rates in India and very limited rural electricity rates. Alternatively, Maharashtra is one of the wealthiest states in India yet has significant electrical deficiencies in parts of the state. Analyzing both Orissa and Maharashtra will help uncover a range of issues that prevent energy access in India. We will analyze barriers to energy access in both states which include, financial constraints on government and citizens, pending land claims, social stratification, limited infrastructure and human resources, educational barriers and socio-economic barriers. These barriers make the expansion of electricity to rural areas a challenge in modern India.

In terms of financial constraints, up front costs of solar power products are one potential barrier. Funding for Solar India is currently planned to take the form of low-interest loans which most individuals in rural India do not qualify for. However, costs for decentralized and off-grid solar lighting systems, run as high as Rs. 7,000 or $152.00 USD for *one* indoor light and solar panel and twice that amount for a two light system, required for most homes. Casual wage labourers, Daliths and subsistence farmers in Orissa earn an average of $1.25 USD a day and the state's GSDP per capita is $436 USD making it difficult to afford such systems. In Maharashtra the GSDP per capita is $1,200.00 USD but much lower for migrant labourers. Although increased energy capacity will provide greater opportunities for income generation (AGECC, 2010), it would still take almost an entire year's salary for most rural families to pay for a two-light system at current costs.

> The major problem of rural consumers is meagre financial resources . . . low propensity to save, domestic debt burden . . . unsatisfactory customer service and intermittent power supply, causing distrust of the utility. SEBs have started using the *franchisee model* to recover costs from consumers in rural areas (Kalra, P. et al, 2007, p. 148).

Due to low wages and annual income rates in rural areas, an electrical franchise such as those utilized throughout Canada and Europe would be more appropriate for rural India. A Franchise can function to reduce up front costs while providing continuous electricity to communities at affordable prices based on their level of usage. An electrical franchise is a service company, such as Vidyut Pratinidhi which provides regular electrical services to consumers with respect to meter reading, billing, and collection (Kalra, P. et al, 2007, p. 148). The consumer pays only the amount of electricity used each month and can adjust electrical usage based on personal affordability and need.

There are currently very limited financing options for de-centralized off or on-grid systems in rural areas, particularly for renewable energy. Alternative financial options include, special payment schemes. For instance, BESCOM, the Bangalore Electricity Supply Company provides a discount of Rs. 50 each month for electrical bills on renewable energy appliances, encouraging residents to switch to renewable electricity.

Land Distribution and Land Claims

Land distribution and land claims are currently an important issue among the Daliths and Tribals of India and they directly relate to energy access. In India "tribal land claims" refer to the land originally owned by Tribals or the first peoples of India based on ancestral occupation. Many "landless peasants" are excluded from national and central government mandates and policies significantly impacting their access to energy. Land claims, land ownership and distribution directly impact access to electricity and all national energy policies. Land claims policies in States such as Orissa correlate with rural energy expansion for two reasons: 1) Individuals who own land in villages are more likely to afford housing, earn an income and thus pay for conventional and non-conventional energy systems boosting electrical access in the village. 2) The mass rejection of territorial land claims in Orissa pose significant barriers to rural advancements in renewable energy expansion as they divert state resources to law suits rather than electrical development.

The Tribals (Aboriginals) differ from Daliths as they tend to inhabit rural areas in the North Eastern States of Arunachal Pradesh, Assam, Manipur, Meghalya, Mizoram, Nagaland, Sikkim and Tripura. The total population of tribals makes up eight percent of India's one billion people. Orissa harbours the third largest population of Tribals in India. As the Aboriginal populations in North America, Tribal populations in India have been denied their land claims for centuries. It has been noted in the State of the world's Aboriginal people Report, that the majority of Aboriginals in India do not have land entitlements although they have occupied the land for generations. In comparison with Aboriginal land claims, however, Indian land claims are exponentially greater in number and rejection. Over 300,000 Tribal land claims were rejected by the government of Orissa in 2008, for instance, because claimants could not provide contractual evidence of inhabiting their land for at least "seventy five years"—exceeding the life expectancy of most Tribals (Jena, 2010). Please see Appendix 2:

Appendix 2: Electrical Access—States in Priority Sequence of Need

Electrical Service: States in Priority Sequence of Need	Percentage of Households with Electricity	Pending Land Claims
1. Bihar		
2. Jarkhand		
3. Orissa		
4. UP	31.9%	
5. North-Eastern States	33.2%	
6. West Bengal	37.5%	
7. Chattisgarh	53.1%	52%
8. MP	70%	Over 50%
9. Rajasthan (higher GSDP than MP)	54.7%	
10. AP (higher GSDP than MP)	67.3%	Over 50%
11. Kerala	70.2%	
12. Tamil Nadu	78.2%	
13. Maharashtra	77.5%	56%
14. Karnataka	78.5%	
15. Gujarat	80.4%	

(RGGVY, 2010)

To prevent the mass rejection of land claims, the Indian Government has put forth "The Forest Rights Act." The Forest Rights Act is meant to help promote land entitlement and legal ownership of land for Tribals. According to Manipadma Jena, the Act "allows claims of individual family titles to already occupied or cultivated forest lands that are currently considered 'encroachments'" (2010). For Daliths, self reliance and sustained development will flow from this type of land ownership and entitlement.

The previous Land Claims Act, "The Tenancy Act," has thus far been ineffective in ensuring property rights and land ownership for tribal communities and Daliths as it has been wrongfully interpreted to confiscate tribal land. Many land claim policies have excluded tribal rights, considering them trivial and low priority. In the 1970s, large portions of communal land were confiscated in the survey and settlement process (Committee, p. 5, 2009). Many cases for land claims have also resulted in the long process of a law suit. Numerous land claims have been denied for unjust reasons. These include:

1. The acquisition of land for urban development such as, highways and mining.
2. Co-lateral Land Alienation caused by climate issues such as pollution, erosion, land damage and mining projects as well as hazardous mining flow from uranium. According to the government committee, often, "alienation of land is pursuant to orders of civil courts which adjudicate revenue matters pertaining to tribal land based on the manipulated records issued by revenue functionaries" (2009, p.9).
3. Defective Surveys of Settlements: Many surveys conducted during the Colonial Period were inaccurate, charting large tracts of community or

tribal land as 'government land' leaving thousands of Orissans without land ownership.

4. Lack of Surveys: In many instances, "Proof of Possession" has not been provided to document ownership of land through the Gram Sabha, a committee advocating on behalf of citizens with land claims cases (2009, p. 5-6).

5. Illegal Permission granted for Purchase of Tribal Land: Illegal Conversion of agricultural land to non-agricultural land has resulted in the misuse and illegal development of preserved agricultural land for highways and urban structures.

6. Gift by Tribals: Tribal land is falsely documented as being "gifted" to the government and other community members.

7. Long Term Leases and Power of Attorney.

8. Manipulation of Records and Boundaries: Misinterpretation and abuse of exemption clauses on land alienation.

9. 'Deemed Reserved Forests' (2009).

On average, there is a 50% land claim rejection rate in every state except for Gujarat. In the states of Assam, Andhra Pradesh, Chattishgarh, Madhya Pradesh and Maharashtra, the percentage of rejected claims is over 50% of the total filed claims. In Madhya Pradesh, for instance, the number of incomplete claims accounts for over 90 percent of the total claims. The percentage of rejected claims is 69 percent in Orissa and 76 percent in Assam.

Caste System and Gender Disparities

Another major setback to poverty reduction through sustainable development in India, and hence to potential electrical expansion, is India's social stratification based on the "caste" system. Of the 1.17 billion people in the country, 200-250 million are classified as the "underclasses," (including Daliths, Tribals and other sub-groups) 80% of whom live below the poverty line. The majority of Daliths and Tribals do not have a paying job or a stable income due in part to discrimination. India has a 33% poverty rate, made mostly of Daliths. Roughly 250, 000 underclasses make up approximately 25% of India's entire 1.17 billion people. The caste system is a socio-political issue that is deeply ingrained in the culture and traditions of modern India, significantly impacting its socio-economic growth. Until the issue of social stratification is appropriately addressed through fundamental and systemic change, it will impede electrical expansion and poverty reduction.

Along with Daliths, very few females are represented in the academic and professional realms due to social constraints on female academic and corporate progression. Significant gender disparities have caused women to make up a very minute percentage of the labour force in Orissa, working mostly as unskilled labourers. Women are unable to gain employment or may lose their jobs causing reductions in public sector growth (UNDP, 2004). Very few females are present in high level, pivotal positions because of limited education, social acceptance, vocational training and domestic obligations. According to Grey, "rural women . . . are the most disadvantaged of all, with least possibility for education and literacy, more daily struggles for sheer survival" (2005, p. 130).

Corruption and Human Resources

Unfortunately, demand for renewable energy products outweighs supply and the local technical expertise required for the Solar India project. For instance, in Orissa alone over 7,000 districts do not have basic electrical access. The population is assessed at 36,706,920 and approximately 46 percent of Orissans live below the poverty line with 93% residing in rural areas. According to the UNDP, 60% of Orissans work as farmers and 75% as casual wage labourers earning an average of one dollar a day. They face a significant lack of employment opportunities and many of the poor in the internal regions of the country depend on forests for their sustenance. Further, they "have limited or no voice in decision making" (UNDP, 2004, p. 5). Vast gender discrepancies are also found in Orissa as a very minute proportion of women are literate and involved in paid labour.

Education

Educational barriers in the states of Maharashtra and Orissa impede the growth and expansion of energy access to rural areas as well. The literacy rate in India has been assessed at 65.3%, 75% for males and 55% for females (Please see Appendix 5). The collective level of educational attainment among the population of the state is a sign of great setbacks and inequality in the functioning of the

Indian education system. In 2001, for instance, the literacy rate in Orissa was 63%-75.35% for males and 50.51% for females. In Maharashtra, the literacy rate was 76.88%-85.97% for males and 67.03% for females (NIC, 2010). These numbers describe not only the rates of illiteracy throughout the country but, more alarmingly, the vast discrepancies of literacy rates between men and women. The literacy rate is between 5-27% higher for males in every state revealing a trend of gender inequality inevitably affecting human development levels (NIC, 2010).

In Mumbai, meanwhile, decline in growth and investment in the electricity sector has contributed to the slow expansion of electrical outreach in rural areas. In a census conducted in 2007, it was found that primary industrial sectors accounted for 1.41% of the Mumbai economy, secondary sectors (manufacturing, construction, electricity*, gas, and water supply) accounted for 28.64% reduced from 36% in 1993-1994 and tertiary sectors (transport, communication, trade, banking, insurance, real estate, business services, and public administration) accounted for 69.95% of the total economy. Consequently fewer manufacturing companies are operating in the field of energy and power as the tertiary sector of business services and communication have seen higher growth rates. According to the UNDP Human Development Report for Mumbai the economic share of the service sector is close to three-fourths of the total, accounting for a large percent of the working population. Growing industries in the service sector include, Telecom, IT, Finance, Tourism, Entertainment, Advertising and Communication (2009). The informal sector (i.e. street vendors) now makes up 36% of the total income generated in the service sector.

Currently, over 47% of the population in greater Mumbai is comprised of interstate migrants (16.19%) carrying both skilled and unskilled credentials. According to the UNDP, "most migration is of the unskilled class" (UNDP, 2009, p. 38) thereby reducing Human Resource potential in the renewable energy sector. Of the total population of casual labourers, self-employed workers and salary-paid employees, only 14% (between the ages of 15-59) were involved in manufacturing, electricity* (UNDP, 2009). There has also been a decline in private sector growth (-1.77%) compared with public sector growth (0.08%) and a decline in total *formal* employment in Mumbai by -0.83% (UNDP, 2009).

Table 1: Socio-Economic Environment for
Energy Services, Maharastra, India

USD (2007-2008)	Maharashtra Economic Outline	India Economic Outline
GSDP	$147,270,000,000 (14% total Indian GDP)- 29th globally	$3,560,000,000,000
GSDP per capita	$1,120.26 (47,051 Rs.)	$3,100.00
Economic growth rate	8.5%	
Population	96,752,247	1,173,108,018
BPL	38,751,451 (40%)	55,975,000,000
Educational Expenditures	4.3% of GSDP	3.2% of GDP
Literacy Rate	76.88%	65.3%
Energy Access initiatives/Policies/ Programs	State Potential: 67,880MW	Average National Production: 723,800,000,000KwH

In Punjab, governments are facing increases in corruption cases. There are currently several hundred legal cases regarding the corruption of the Punjab government. This is hampering economic growth. For instance, there are 40,000 individuals with BA degrees who do not currently have jobs in the Punjab. There are human resource defecits in the education and health sectors. The debt in Punjab has also increased to $75,000 crores with a payment of $8,000 crores each year. The Peoples Party of Punjab is looking to modernize Punjab's and India's way of thinking to match western states. The younger generations are looking to re-define the political climate and increase east-west cooperation with a focus on freedom, rule of law and economic prosperity.

Table 2: Socio-Economic Environment
for Energy Services, Orissa

USD	Orissa Economic Outline
GSDP	$29,670,000,000 (2.99%)
GSDP per capita	$436.95 (26,654Rs.)
Economic Growth Rate (2004)	3-4%
Population	36,706,920
BPL	16,885,183 (46%) (*Tendulkar Report)
Educational Expenditures	5%-GSDP (2004)
Literacy Rate	63.1% (2001) Male: 75% Female: 51%
Renewable Energy Access	State Potential: 4500MW
Total Cost for State Energy Access	56,091 villages and hamlets: $16,827,300,000 (5.6% of GSDP)
HDI	11th out of 15 major states (UNDP, 2004)

Chapter 6

Field Work in Karnataka

Universe

Each entity in our universal tree
Carries within its temporal frame,
An energy we cannot see
Without form, figure or shape.

A soul, I say, a spirit within
A light so bright it'd blind our eyes
An abyss of endless love and bliss
With which we create what we surmise.

This place, this ocean of eternal light
Connects all in one, one in all
As branches connect all leaves and vines
And the swaying sea connects all land.

When discovered within we see
Its depths of love fathomless be,
As the far reaches of inifinity,
This energy allows us to fly free.

Promoting Equality Based Socio-Economic Growth and Learning throughout India one Village at a Time

Through research in solar energy, we hope to discover not only the potential and capacity of renewable energy in India to improve documented human development figures, but also funding alternatives that can help improve affordability of renewable energy appliances for rural and urban populations living below the poverty line. This research aims to explore government and civil involvement in energy access, financing options and technological innovations to help reduce up-front costs particularly for solar photovoltaic energy. It provides suggestions for electrical expansion in India by noting current barriers in the field and how to overcome those barriers. Highlighting regional and global figures and cross-comparisons of socio-economic growth, this study also aims to highlight the advantages of renewable energy and its relationship to human development conditions in India. It focuses on providing information on sustainable development and the use of renewable energy in the rapidly developing urban centres of India, in order to help global efforts in reducing climate change through the goals set out in the Solar India project.

Working in the Field

During my graduate field work, I spent the majority of my time gathering extensive primary and secondary research information for a document report on energy access investigating:

- Barriers to energy access in Orissa and Maharashtra

- Stakeholders in the energy access debate
- Policy environment in Orissa and Maharashtra
- Financial Institutions Environment
- HR Environment in Orissa and Maharashtra

Research in Solar Lighting and Renewable Energy involved the following work activities at Solar Electric Light Company (SELCO): Reading literature and materials on global benefits of renewable energy; Learning about the "Solar India" mission and identifying three key phases of the national project for decentralized, off-grid renewable energy systems; Researching information on the renewable energy potential in various constituencies of India and the World; Gathering research data on the various types of renewable energies such as, wind, solar, hydro, geo-thermal, and biomass; Interviews with key government officials including:

1.) The Karnataka Renewable Development Limited in Bangalore, India.
2.) BESCOM: Bangalore Electricity Supply Company.
3.) Ministry of Rural Development in New Delhi, India.

In conducting the research, I visited the Rural Electrification Corporation, the Electrical Supply Company of Karnataka and the Karnataka Renewable Energy Development Ltd; I also visited the Ministry of Rural Development in Delhi, the Office of the Prime Minister. I spoke also with a number of electrical and mechanical engineers at SELCO during my internship. They provided me with essential technical information and national trends in development with regards to energy expansion in the State. As I discovered the need for marketing management and innovation are key in energy expansion as many rural families are unaware of service providers such as, SELCO and available government subsidies.

Further, in conducting field projects with The Society for the Deprived Classes Education—installing solar power in the Karnataka State children's home and in a remote rural village in Andhra Pradesh called Ambavaram, I noted the great need for electricity in rural areas of the state.

Karnataka State Children's Home

My initial field project took place in the Karantaka State children's home in Bangalore. Here, we installed four solar LED lights in the main hall and two solar lights in the kitchen with a large solar panel. While teaching in the children's home for three months, I facilitated a variety of lessons for the children. We brought the children prizes, art materials, stationary, reading materials, sports equipment and writing supplies to promote literacy and sports activities. However, the children were never as overjoyed as they were following the installation of solar lighting. It was as though they felt they held a sense of importance. Realising that they would no longer need to live in darkness in the evenings. They would be safe at night with emergency lighting available if needed. Ultimately, safety had been prioritized through the installation of the solar lighting. The superintendent and the students also described the benefits of the solar lighting during power outages, dinner time and evening recreational activities.

Society for the Deprived Classes Education

During my field placement, I also worked with the Society for Deprived Classes Education on projects involving slum dwellers school projects in Bangalore, and rural development for the Lazarouth Work Therapy Centre and school in Andhra Pradesh.

In terms of my field work with the Society for the Deprived Classes Education I visited slum schools in Richmond Town, Bangalore and interviewed children and teachers from the slum community. I gathered Primary and Secondary Research Data: I collected secondary data by researching trends in renewable energy and rural development in Andhra Pradesh. As a preliminary step for the project and as advised by my site supervisor, Mr. Kathary, I visited the Ministry of Rural Development in New Delhi to speak with personal secretary and assistant of Rural Development Minister, Agatha Sangama. With them, I discussed development plans in Ambavaram, Andhra Pradesh and delivered informational material about the Ambavaram project—Phase 1 of the project is to expand the Senior Citizen Work Therapy Centre namely to prepare one acre of land and provide water supply for land cultivation. Phase two is to prepare five acres of land for cultivation. Phase three is to utilize five acres of land for the purpose of growing fruit trees such as, mango, orange, lime and tamarind within a fenced area. Phase four of the work plan is to create a bore well for water irrigation and build a wall around the land to prevent soil erosion.

During my interviews with entrepreneurs at the Canada Pacific Gateway, I learned about leading bio-fuel technology. I was informed by business associates there that the seeds of the jatrofa plant can be sold to the State government for bio-fuel processing. Further, I learned about planting methods for Jatrofa and Hongue seeds from the University of Agricultural Sciences. I then gathered work supplies to Implement Phase 1 of Ambavaram Village

Project: 1.) Jatrofa and Honge seeds; 2.) Jatrofa plants from Lal Bagh National Park; 3.) Solar lamp post and 4 LED lights from SELCO 4.) Water Pump; Meeting with key officials for approval of development work in Andhra Pradesh including: 1.) Mandalam Revenue Officer; 2.) Development Officer; 3.) Land Development Officer. Field Work and Implementation of Research work Plan:

1) Education: teaching lessons and learning activities to children in the village school.
2) Lighting: installation of solar lighting on school premises
3) Land cultivation: planting Jatrofa and Hongue seeds.
4) Irrigation: Water pump installation and creation of water tank
5) Composting: constructing a compost for organic waste materials

Ambavaram Village Project

The second and largest field visit was in Ambavaram village, Andhra Pradesh. Ambavaram village is a remote rural village located in Eastern India in a state called Andhra Pradesh. The project we organized was initially researched and presented to the government of Andhra Pradesh by the Society for the Deprived Classes Education. We funded phase 1 of this project by fundraising through LFC as the society was not able to fully implement the project. The village project was set out by the Society two years earlier. However, they had not yet received funding from the Ministry of rural development to carry out the project. We installed three solar LED lights in a school in

Ambavaram village, one LED light in the Church and one outdoor lamp post. We stayed in Ambavaram for nearly a week during phase 1 of the project. One evening, we experienced a power outage in the village and the only lights working were the solar lights we had installed. Many of the villagers came to the school house (where we were residing) and shared the evening with us talking about the lighting and trends in education, dreams and aspirations they had. They were overjoyed to see that the lights in the Church and the school were still working even during a power outage so they could have their evening church service and have a secure place for shelter. Many of the villagers used candles to light their small homes during the outage. Since then, the State government in Andhra Pradesh published a press release regarding the need for solar lighting in all new residential and commercial buildings. There have been new building construction projects in Mallepalle (nearest city to Ambavaram) utilizing solar lighting.

Shishu Mandir

Shishu Mandir is a student centre comprised of a children's home for neglected and abandoned children. It includes a children's vocational and training centre as well as an educational centre for elementary and high school aged children from underprivileged backgrounds. A Children's Home is being commissioned by Dr. Hella Mundra of Germany, with eco-friendly design and solar lighting for Daliths in eastern Karnataka

Chapter 7

Food Security

Achieving Food Security and Energy Access through
Sustainable Development in Rural India

(By: Vanessa Louise Goodall):

Since the liberalisation of India's economy in the 1990s, this state has experienced unprecedented economic growth. Today, based upon Purchasing Power Parity (PPP) India has the world's fourth largest economy (following China, Japan and the USA), boasting an average economic growth rate of 6% per year (averaged between 1991 and 2009) and a GDP per capita of $3,354 (PPP USD) (Murthy, 2009, p, 55). Compared to previous decades, in which India's GDP per capita stood at $1,050 (PPP US) (1987) and $2,077 (PPP USD) (2000).

However, in contrast to these economic gains, India has been unable to simultaneously increase human development along with that of economic development. According to the 2010 Human Development Index (HDI), published by the United Nations Development Programme (UNDP), India currently ranks 119th of the 169 surveyed countries. Although, this is an improvement in comparison to the 2007/08 HDI report, in which India ranked 126th of the 177 surveyed countries, India's low HDI score is a result of the chronic persistence of human insecurities such as gender inequality, illiteracy, high rates of maternal and infant mortality, hunger and poverty. Unlike the top three world economies of China, Japan and the USA, whose HDI scores denote a higher level of human development than India (89th, 11th and 4th out of 169 surveyed countries for 2010), economic liberalisation has translated into relatively better livelihood indicators for citizens of those states based upon the HDI survey.

For the citizens of India, this disparity between economic and human development has translated into endemic poverty for millions (World Bank, 2010). With a population of 1,173,108,018 (July 2010), 75.6% live on less than $2.00 PPP US per day and 41.6% live below the international poverty line[1] of $1.25 PPP US per day (2010) (CIA Factbook, 2010, India; HDI, 2010, India; World Bank, 2011, para. 2; UNDP, 2010, para. 3). As a result, 40% of the world's undernourished children live in India, as do 25% of the world's hungry poor (World Food Program, 2010, India). Of this, 43.5% of children in India under the age of five are malnourished, 47.9% of children under the age of five have stunted growth, and half of all pregnant women (ages 15-49), approximately 75% of children under the age of five suffer iron deficiency anaemia[2] (WFP, 2008, p. 5) and, "one million children die every year for lack of food" (Shiva & Jalees, 2009, p. 2).

In addition, India has a maternal mortality rate of 450 deaths per 100,000 live births, a child mortality rate (under the age of five) of sixty nine deaths per 1,000 live births and a life expectancy of 64.4 years. In comparison to the global averages of these statistics, standing at 273 maternal deaths for every 100,000 live births, approximately sixty deaths (under the ages of five) for every 1,000 children born and a life expectancy of 69.3 years, it is perplexing to see a country of such economic power, to suffer such poor human development indicators (HDI, 2010, p. 146, 160, 201).

Identifying the root causes behind human insecurity in India is a complex challenge. A country of many cultures, religious traditions, languages, histories, regional influences, and environmental and social landscapes, the root causes of the mentioned human insecurities in

India are the result of a series of interdependent factors. These factors include the continual impact of colonisation, the caste system, an inefficient bureaucratic system, corruption, a lack of basic and effective infrastructure, extreme gender inequalities, internal and regional conflicts, poor education[3], climate change[4] and the high price of fossil fuels[5]. According to Dr. Shiva, Navdanya's founder,

In summary, these factors have disenfranchised 400 million farm households, 160 rural landless, 64 million urban households and 56 million herders, fishers and forest dependent Indians (Shiva & Jalees, 2009, p. 1). Furthermore, these factors disproportionally impact Indians from the states of Madhya Pradesh, Chhattisgarh, Jharkhand, Bihar, Orissa, Uttar Pradesh and Rajasthan who together [harbour] 43% of India's hungry children (Shiva, 2009, p. 44). [6]

Chapter 8

The Pivotal Role of Government

During my interview with the Secretary to the Minister of Rural Development, I learned that energy expansion is a pertinent issue for the central government of India, however, water irrigation and enhanced agricultural production are also important areas on the government agenda. Further, in order to qualify for subsidies, State's must apply to the central government with an application for energy expansion. This is typically a long and arduous but necessary process.

In terms of policy development for renewable energy expansion specifically in the state of Orissa, I was told by a number of solar energy engineers such as Ananth Aravamudan and Siddarth Kumar that subsidies are inefficient as they rarely reach individuals on the ground. Further, there is a lack of policy development helping to mainstream sustainable technologies. There is also an absence of incentives from the government for renewable energy expansion. Further, at SELCO I learned that 115 million primary aged children do not attend school worldwide partly due to limited energy access. In addition, I learned that many farmers lose thousands of kilograms of their produce due to the lack of appropriate refrigeration systems and communication with city markets. SELCO's ultimate objective is to improve agriculture, education, water sanitation and irrigation and livelihood generation through innovative solutions in energy access. By creating solar energy entrepreneurs and solar energy manufacturers throughout India, it hopes to improve trends in energy access as well as other development sectors. SELCO not only creates ideas in solar home lighting but also solar water heaters and solar cookers. They seek to improve quality of life for low-income households through increased work hours and productivity. As a need based solution provider,

SELCO works closely with commercial and rural banks to finance sustainable energy systems for the underserved.

Some progress in the renewable energy sector is being made. According to the Karnataka Renewable Energy Development Lmt., the state of Karnataka currently has cumulative generation of biomass, small hydro, wind and co-generation of 20,740MW (2010). The KREDL enjoys a trusting and accountable relationship with the central government and thus almost 78.8% of households in Karnataka have electricity. The KREDL applies for subsidies and grants for Renewable energy projects and has been very effective in successfully implementing projects.

In terms of States such as, Andhra Pradesh, however, the situation is quite different. Only 67% of households have electricity. According to Mr. George Henry Katary, school teacher and social worker, Dalith households in rural Andhra Pradesh suffer greatly from the lack of development and education. He and his wife have donated about eleven acres of their ancestral land to the Daliths of Ambavaram village to promote education and welfare among the people. They have also built a school for the villagers; however, they are not able to find full time educators to teach the children. The process of land development taken on by Mr. Katary and the Society for Deprived Classes Education is: 1) Land development 2) water irrigation 3) renewable energy installation. During our field visit, myself and other interns were able to help with these three phases and we saw great improvements in the morale of the people.

In terms of educational progress of Daliths in urban and rural areas, the trends are worrisome. According to Hella Mundra, foundress of Shishu Mandir Children's Home and Education Centre in Bangalore, Dalith children often do not receive the opportunities presented to children from other backgrounds. However, with a high level education, their career options multiply. An example of this is a child who grew up at Shishu Mandir Home, Viji. She completed her degree in software engineering and she is now working as a teacher. Two other girls, Deepa and Reshma, completed their degrees and are working for the CS medical institute in Karnataka as nurses.

During my internship with the Society for the Deprived Classes Education, the Children's Home and SELCO-India, I realised that India has faced a lot of changes in terms of economic growth since my last visit in 2008. The inflation rate across the country, for instance, is 10% causing food insecurity and increased poverty in most areas. Inflation rates in India have increased food prices, education and tuition fees, housing and health care prices resulting in reduced human security. I have realised also, that the importance of attaining energy access is a stepping stone for advancements in health care, agriculture, education and human shelter. I learned upon my arrival in India, that most rural communities are not able to provide young children with a proper education due to inefficiencies in basic infrastructure and energy access. Until this infrastructure is put in place, societal growth will be minimal in most rural communities.

Unfortunately, with the rise in inflation, an increase in wages has not followed suit. Most public employees suffer from a lack of affordability and reduced savings. A domestic worker at my home stay in Bangalore, for instance, caught a severe influenza virus during my stay. She was 8 months pregnant and at risk of losing her child for the third time (she suffered two miscarriages previously). As most Daliths, her and her husband could not afford the medical admittance at the hospital, required for her illness. However, myself and my host family covered her medical costs. She was admitted in the ICU for three days following an eight hour wait in emergency. She made a full recovery, however, the medical costs were about Rs. 3000 ($60 CAD). If she had not been admitted she may have lost her third child. Other low-income families, due in part to multidimensional poverty, do not have the means or the assistance to receive appropriate medical treatment and they often face higher risk of miscarriage, infant mortality, and chronic illness from minor ailments.

At this phase, India's development has three key priorities: 1) rural electrification of all villages and hamlets through sustainable development and renewable energy 2) land ownership and social equality 3) Increased human security and health care. From a renewable energy standpoint, I have realised the importance of non-conventional energy in India's overall development. Many schools and households in India today do not have internal lighting, reducing productivity in a multitude of areas such as, employment, household care, and general security. Students in rural areas are often unable to study after the school day due to the lack of lighting at home.

In order for Solar India and other minor and major governmental energy projects to be successful, however, a united government platform is required. Indian government agencies have the political will, economic strength and the expertise to implement action plans for solar energy production and distribution--and it is their responsibility to do so. It is a collective challenge and must be met by a collective solution.

Government support structures, pooled resources and expertise can help to build much needed infrastructure such as information databases and renewable energy parks. These, in turn, can be implemented to reduce deficiencies in energy access and improve quality of life for the majority of citizens. Health care, agricultural production, education, employment opportunities and socio-economic development will flourish only from investments in foundational infrastructural development such as, grid-based renewable energy technologies. Solar energy, in particular, has the potential to provide long term sustainable electricity to households with few costs attached following installation. In every state that I visited, I have experienced power outages and fragmented electricity. Irregularity in energy supply indicates the great need for refinement in policies and actions dedicated to the promotion of efficient energy systems.

In terms of social equality and resource distribution, land claims in states such as, Orissa, Maharashtra and Andhra Pradesh need to be legally assessed and accounted for. Tribal lands belonging to indigenous groups, equitable land ownership and distribution is fundamental to the Indian development program. Historically, much of the rich and productive community land has been taken by the government and wealthy farmers. Also, during the survey and settlement process occurring every 25-30 years, "land grabbing by powerful individuals, facilitated by leveraging over settlement officers, appears to be commonplace...the net effect is to systematically discriminate against the rural poor and the socially excluded" (Mearns & Sinha, 1999, p. 5). Socio-economic equity in development will occur when fair and just legal practices in land allocation take place.

Providing universal energy access will pose a number of critical challenges related to overcoming gaps in the local institutional capacity and governance required to produce, deliver, manage, operate and maintain these solutions (AGECC, 2010).

With open lines of communication all 28 states and 420 districts of India can achieve universal energy access in rural and urban settings. Mandatory electrical expansion of underserved areas of India through the application of roof-top solar power panels, hydro-powered Single Wire Earth Return, or photo-voltaic energy options in a customer-use model can occur in a timely and efficient manner with appropriate financing options.

In the same way, solar power can be harnessed and distributed on a large scale from solar power plants. In Seville Spain, for instance, a solar power plant harnesses over 11MW of energy by concentrating solar energy on the top portion of a 115m tower from a solar receiver and turbine made from 624 large movable mirrors (120 square meters each). The tower then distributes power to various homes and communities within Seville (Power Technology, 2011).

Auroville

In terms of cost effective production of solar power cells using materials such as, copper and mirrors can also be used to capture the sun's energy in a cost effective manner. In the solar kitchen located in Auroville, India for instance, the solar power dish is composed of small mirrors which concentrate the sun's energy to power the operation as well as neighbouring structures. The solar kitchen operates twenty four hours completely reliant on solar radiation for power supply. Auroville has over 150 houses powered by photovoltaic energy and 50 households which use grid-connected solar power. The total solar photovoltaic capacity in Auroville is over 15% of the total solar capacity in India (Auroville, 2010). Auroville is a community of 2,237 people located in Eastern Tamil Nadu, which have experimented with a multitude of architectural and energy innovations to promote sustainable living.

As a governmental priority, such capacities can be installed in rural areas within the next two years with the assistance of domestic renewable energy experts such as, the Rural Electrification Corporation of India, the Ministry of Rural Development, solar experts in Auroville, SELCO and international energy experts from countries such as, China and Singapore which have achieved universal energy access.

Finance

Micro-financing options can be made available to individual households, new companies and institutions by national banks or private donors. Micro-finance loans can help finance micro-projects such as, home lighting and water heating systems as well as macro-projects such as, solar power parks. Direct financing from the central government and concerned states will be required for the employment of needed trained personnel and suppliers. Electrical capacity should be extended to states in a prioritized and objective manner by the government. Also, Foreign Direct Investment (FDI) should be targeted and measurable in order to achieve energy capacity in a particular hamlet, village, community or rural district within a given time frame. The priority sequencing of state-based electrical expansion may be based on 1.) The Percentage of households with electricity and 2.) GSDP: Gross State Domestic Product. (Please see Appendix 3).

Direct Economic Investment

Successful large-scale electrification programmes are underpinned by government targets and priorities that inform a rigorous planning process, legislation and regulation. (UN, AGECC, 2010).

If they do qualify, many are not able to afford the monthly payments. Thus, loans should remain the last financing option for energy access. Instead, direct Government Expenditure in the form of grants are needed to fund relevant projects (for individuals, entrepreneurs, researchers, companies and NGOs dedicated to renewable energy manufacturing and installation), internal infrastructural aid (building solar power parks, constructing vocational and polytechnic institutions in rural areas to train rural inhabitants in solar power and green energy) and educational scholarships. For example, the Central Government of India, in conjunction with the State governments in question, may plan to fund the installation of 100,000 solar LED lights in rural districts of Bihar and Orissa by 2011 through the human resource support of a solar power company. The company will be provided the full amount of manufacturing, installation and HR costs for the project so long as project goals and quotas are met within a given time frame.

Recommendations for Orissa

Orissa requires legal action and implementation of the Forest Claims Act in order to provide land claims to original inhabitants of tribal and indigenous land--making energy access an affordable option for Tribals and other low income families. As a State which is proportionately more rural than urban, electrical expansion in Orissa requires the implementation of one of two strategic plans of action to achieve State-wide electricity. The first, most cost-effective and timely strategy requires hydro-powered single phase or Single Wire Earth Return supplied by the Rural Electrification Corporation of Orissa. Electricity must be implemented in an urgent manner during the initial development phase in order to alleviate the stress and living anxiety experienced by individuals who do not have electricity in the home. Electricity will be provided by State and municipal utilities funded through the Ministry of New and Renewable Development on a sequential basis to the most remote and underserved households and regions first. From an engineering perspective, extending electrical capacity through mini-grid systems providing decentralized solar power in a prioritized sequence to high need areas first. The second strategic option is mandated, widespread installation of off-grid, or mini grid centralized or decentralized roof top solar lighting systems on all "new" and unelectrified buildings in rural and urban areas using LED or CFL lights.

Further, Orissa has over 19,000 square kilometers of underdeveloped regions, constituting 12.17% of its total geographical area. These land areas can be developed in renewable energy capacities such as, solar power parks, wind mill parks, jatrofa plant harvesting for bio-fuel production, or rain water harvesting sites to produce renewable energy and water for irrigation supplied to Orissa and sold to other parts of India. These regions have received over Rs. 182,000,000 for development from the central government to date. Creating a solar power plant in such areas is a highly efficient investment and an appropriate use of the land which would otherwise be wasted. Solar power plants have the potential of capturing large amounts (over 1MW) of solar energy and feeding it back into the grid or selling it to neighbouring states.

Inter-State Training Campaigns

In addition, to strengthen the economy, promoting industrial growth and agriculture in India extending invitations to economists, engineers, manufacturing specialists, and agriculturalists from other States within India to train locals and set up infrastructure within rural India would be highly beneficial. Funding for specific and goal-oriented programs can come directly from Solar India financing schemes on the basis of a bidding or blind selection process—selection would be based on systematic criteria found in the Paris Declaration and the proven credentials of applicants. Criteria for rural development programs would include: sustainability following the withdrawal of experts in the field as well as energy efficiency. All projects would require assessment at the end of the term and project leaders will be held accountable to their initial objectives providing the results of their individual mission in the field. Thus, Solar India will be a national mission comprised of specific, measurable, achievable, realistic, and timed (SMART) missions:

- Specific: The project goal should have a specific objective or outcome.
- Measurable: The project achievements should be measurable.
- Achievable: Goals should be achievable considering the geographic region, technology, climate, human resources and costs involved.
- Realistic: The objectives should be applicable and appropriate for the project and region considering the availability of funding and resources.
- Time-Scale Appropriate: The time scale for the project should be monitored and the project should be completed within the given time frame.

Socio-Economic Solutions for Rural India

In terms of creating socio-economic stability in rural India, Territorial land claims entitled to tribal and rural communities within rural India should be rectified in a linear and transparent manner. Rural India will also benefit from immediate rural infrastructure such as, solar powered water pumps, water tanks, bore wells, tractors and transportation routes for agricultural production and price management. The creation of government-funded vocational training institutes and public education systems which reduce "regional gender disparities" are needed to initiate and sustain economic growth. Further economic solutions include: Broad-based labor intensive economic growth; Mobilization of higher resources; Diversification of livelihoods of groups from lower socio-economic backgrounds; higher agricultural growth; Institutional credit and grants and the sustainable Management of forests (UNDP, 2004).

According to Wuyuan Peng and Jiahua Pan, researchers in energy and sustainable development, the most efficient management of electricity occurs at the county or village level. However, before this can take place, regulations and policies must be in place. They further state the importance of government involvement and funding as well as investment by rural people themselves (2006) used in the Chinese electrification scheme. Three major changes have taken place by the Chinese government: 1) "Rural electricity had a separate administrative system from the urban areas. 2) From 1949 to 1977, China established a... vertical system of rural electricity administration under strict central planning. 3) At the end of the 1970s...the central government handed over the management of the local electricity system to local government" (2006, p. 71). As rural areas are the back bone of the Solar India project, it would be beneficial for it to operate through the RGGVY or another rural administrative branch.

Gill's Grandfather Parmanand Singh (right) in family
home, Vancouver with family friend, Pakhar Singh.

Gill with her father, Amarjit, brother, Deepak,
Pakhar Singh, and her Grandfather, 1988

Gurpavan in Ambavaram Village, Mallepalle, Andhra Pradesh with village inhabitants during a field visit to install solar panels in the village school, church, senior citizen work therapy centre and outdoor common area.

Ambavaram Village, Mallepalle, Andhra Pradesh--village children helping to install solar lighting for security purposes through the Lotus Foundation for Children (LFC).

Part II

Intimations of Equality and Human Harmony

The sun and the moon are lamps of incomparably beautiful light. Throughout the world, the Infinite Light is pervading.[5]

Lunar Sea

The sea at sunset is a site sublime
  Dressed as an empress by the sun swept eve
    In graceful robes of celestial light
      Brushed by the wind's gentle breeze
      In glory of the coming night

    Laying humbly below the mountains
    Shining by the paint of the saffron sky
Kssed by earth's fiery shades
    Proudly revealing its laughing tide
      Swaying endlessly in its velvet veil.

The setting sun departs with approval
  Blessing the sea's adorned brow,
      Clears the palette for the moon's arrival.
      Preparing the sky for sundown,
        It turns its cheek and darkness falls

      At twilight the solemn sea calls for the moon
    In sweet song of longing and desire
For the moon to immerse in its oceanic tune
    To become one with its depths of life
        Eternally illuminating its visage of blue

The moon so intoxicated with love it bleeds
Sprinkling the sea nymph with jewels of light
With lucent beams carrying cosmic dreams
Clothing it in gauzy white
Alas, with silver beads, crowning it the lunar queen

Beholding the sea in all its glory
The moon begs for the tide to rise
Hoping to have a closer eye
At the beauty of its flawless brine
Speaking in love, through the stars, the silent lunar night

In ardour every night the moon does, the sea thus seek

May 24, 2007

**The Earth, a droplet,
in the cosmic ocean.**

On a magnificent rainbow I saw in the early days of December. There were not one but two rainbows one above the other—the brightest I have ever seen. One half of the sky was dark with thick grey clouds and rain, while the other half was alight with blue sky and gleaming sunshine.

Bridge

As the concrete bridge of man
Connects two divided lands
The pristine rainbow entwines
Nature's opposing strands

Thus uniting grey and light
Rain and sun, dark and day
Dreary clouds and sunlit highs
Hope and dismay holding hands

This painted bridge sings a song
Of peace, harmony and love
Between all colours of earth
And all colours of our lives

It displays itself, a grand site
Brightest when a darker day
Is met with a brighter sky
Proving that rain and sun create a grand display

As friends and lovers they unite
To create a splendour of light
Existing everlasting in our minds
Reminding us to find love in life

Water and fire
May reign alone with glory
But together
Create beauty ever growing

Unity

They say that love exists
In the union of two
In hearts it does persist
Remains, if bonds are true

They say that love is bliss
When walking hand in hand
And, if two lovers kiss
Life is sweet as song

But what if there is more
Past love of eyes, lips and touch
And beyond lovers' lore
That which is felt untouched

Experienced in faculties
Used less commonly
Floating within inner seas
Abyssal caves of destiny

A sense of harmony
Within the soul, the self
With every soul and being
At peace . . . with all that is—feel unity

Not only with the one
With every utter breath
Everything afloat
Upon this blessed earth

Energy

Energy is all we are
All that is
Is light and dark
True and false
Only this persists
The love we share
Our thoughts and joys
Make us what we are
They add light and hope
To brighten days
Colour all realms
With rhythmic songs
If our thoughts be dark
Dark too is life
All that surrounds
Painted with strife
What's within
Grows to produce
The life we live
We do reap what we sow

sas dheep anoop joth thri bhavan joth apaar ||[6]

There is only one breath of life;
We are all made of the same clay.

The light within all is the same;
One Light pervades all beings

The light intermingles with them,

But it is not obscured, remaining constant and pure

Chapter 9

Waheguru—Beautiful Lord

God

God is as clear as water
As free as the breeze
As bright as sunlight
As pure as its rays
As fresh as new leaves
As still as the trees
As soft as sand
Impenetrable as rock
As vast as the universe
As steady as the seas
As swift as lightning
As silent as night
As fierce as the eagle
As light as the air
As smooth as ice
As hot as fire
As endless as a sphere
As Beautiful as the spectrum of light
As artistic as the skies
God is His creation
Know His work—
Know Him

My Guru

Your gifts are countless
Your words divine
Your way is wondrous
Your breath is life

Truth is God

Mahatma Gandhi once said, "Truth is God . . ."
I reflected and considered this thought:

Truth sings in the wings of great raptors
Truth is rhythm . . . breath
Truth is the heart beat
Truth glides in the flight of brave souls

Truth dances on the rays of the sun
It glows in the heart of the great star
It warms all shapes of earth
It gleams on every face

Truth is etched in the essence of who we are
It is ingrained in every atom of creation
Truth is the thread by which we are stitched
Indeed, Truth is God.

As the Sun

Is it He or She or It or Them
The one or many who stitched life's hem
Is the Creator formless or with form
Is Waheguru as the sun is or human in form?

I believe that the Creator is....

As the Sun

He who stitched life's hem
Weaved beginning to end
Tailored both women and men
Can be witnessed through the sun's trends

As the sun exists so does He
A single entity
Yet in its entirety
Equally reaching every being

As the sun, He gives life and takes it away
He illuminates both night and day
Changes the months from April to May
And paints the sky from blue to gray

As the sun, the Lord is the essence of life
Without which we cannot exist
Without which we will not persist
A life without the Lord is a life without light

So let Waheguru be the reigning light in your life

Open Door

God, the door to your Truth
The gate of knowledge
Is open to all
No one is turned away

All who wish to know
Are welcomed in your court
Every soul sits in brilliance
In a radiance unique

A seat is reserved forever
For each a place their own
A sanctuary where they dwell
Where fear does not flow

Let me enter that gate,
Where, in your grace,
Harmony and peace persist
And, one unifying force prevails

Let me open that door
From which none
Are turned away
Where every soul finds peace

Where all are welcomed
All are viewed the same
Sitting on equal ground
Where we drink tea of tranquility

Sit on thrones of humility
Eat fruit of contentment
Where love is wealth, kind words are jewels
Let me sit in God's court

Where all are graceful
Flowers in the field of life

Moment

Every moment
That I face
I will live with your grace
As each moment
That does pass
May be my last

2008

Universe

As the river
Falls into the ocean
And becomes the ocean

Living creatures
Fall into death
And become the universe

Rejoice

I do not know
If this is the right way
If I walk
On the destined path
Only time will reveal

Still I will live and rejoice
For the breath and the life
Instilled within me
For the mind and the soul
For the flesh and the will

I will **rejoice**

Spirit Pure

I have felt the Spirit pure
Breathe into this earthly form
With such power and such strength
As our life's beating pulse
It is calm and at ease

A silent shore
Filled with glee
A creative force
Of ecstasy

As graceful as a sea of stars
Bright as our glaring sun
As vibrant as our beating hearts
Pure as our glacial peaks
It is calm and at ease

Love, peace and harmony
The essence of our source
Truth, light and humility
Are the faces of its mould
It is calm and at ease

Every lively breathe
Forms new bonds, new birth and form
Each breath, a new dream
A new miracle performed
When the tide of our lives

Is calm and at ease
The gifts of universal light
Are clear for us to see
Live in peace within yourselves,
Let no ill enter your worlds

Chapter 10

Mother

"Of woman are we born, of woman conceived; to woman engaged, to woman married. Women are befriended, by woman the civilization is continued. When a woman dies, woman is sought. It is by woman that the entire social order is maintained. Then why call her evil? From her, kings are born." (Guru Nanak Dev Ji)

Woman of Earth

Tilled, raked, awakened to create
The earth is sown with nascent seeds
Watered, warmed, weaved by nature
Instilling life, fruit, and dreams to reap

So too a woman's womb
Is earth, is soil, is fertile ground
Where seeds are planted in union
Nurtured by love, by care, by joy

Earth and womb are full of life
Full of worth enriching
Delicate forms to inspire
The glory of creation

As seeds of earth, seeds of the womb
Grow strong where the air is calm
Where rain drips in even pockets
And sustenance easily found

Those seeds grow taller after birth
Which face temperate weathers
Seeds which enjoy both sun and rain
But not one more than the other

As the earth holds in place
All seeds which she has raised
They stand tall upon her face
Held by her steady grace

Women too, nurture the roots
Of their tender seeds
Not only until the birth
But throughout their earthly days

Such is the bond
Of the mother and seed
In separation it strengthens
The two are one indeed

Our Great Mother Earth

Woman

She is
One who loves
From her
Soul of souls
In her
Heart of hearts
Those who
Treat her kind
Will reap
Every benefit
She will
Sacrifice
All she has
For those who wait
Who know
Her caring ways

Seed

Seeds are sown in many fields
By those who wish to touch the earth
Plowing through fertile dirt
They wait until the field is sweet

And then unleash heaps of seeds
In hopes that they will grow
Manifold moulds of gold
And so the earth is creased

Not all seeds will sprout
Not all buds will bloom
Only those carressed
Yield sweetened fruit

Love what you do sow
If you do not know
It will not grow
Love and it will show

Mother

As the earth is sown
So is she
With seeds of souls
To create

As the earth nurtures
So does she
Caring for young endlessly
As a beating heart

As the earth rewards
So does she
With new birth
For all to see

As the earth sustains
So does she
Caring for children in every age
Sharing their dreams

As the earth does love
so does she
Her heart is one with her child
For them she breathes

Global Village

Within this village upon the globe
So many live in constant search
For food to feed body and soul
For the path of Truth upon the earth

They say food is plenty upon the land
They say the soul must find itself
So why do so many stand
Without a morsel upon their shelves

And without purpose for their sullen souls
I have seen them wander with no direction
In utter confusion
Feeding on that which kills not creates

To ease their heavy hearts
Should not the rich in wealth
Feed the poor and mend their hearts
Should not the rich in soul

Share their insights
To help the lost escape such strife
And find paths of Truth and light
Welcoming day not bitter night

Chapter 11

The Power of Love

Love (Corintheans 4:8)

"Love endures long and is patient and kind; love never is envious nor boils over with jealousy or hautily. It is not conceited, arrogant and inflated with pride. It is not rude (unmannerly) and does not act unbecomingly, love, God's love in us does not insist on its own rights or its own way, for it is not self-seeking; it is not touchy, fretful or resentful; it takes no account of the evil done to it (it pays no attention to a suffered wrong). It does not rejoice in injustice and unrighteiousness, but rejoices when right and Truth prevail. Love bears up with everything and anything that comes. It is ever ready to believe the best of every person, its hopes are fadeless under all circumstances and it endures everything without weakening. Love never fails (never fades out or becomes obsolete or comes to an end)."

There is power in love. Through love, all things can be achieved. The greatest test is to master love for oneself. When we love ourselves unconditionally, we connect with the beauty of the universe and the world. We discover that the thread of Truth sewn throughout every atom of existence is sewn too within us. Self love allows us to discover the vastness of the creation—our depths are a microcosm of the depths of the universe. Each time we journey within we have the opportunity to discover another mountain, valley, cave or crevice within each abounds deep pockets of love.

Heart

The earth is the sky
The sky the earth
All is in all intertwined
The globe, a sole beating heart

Formed in pristine nebulas
Stars, the dreams,
Inspiring the universe
Glimmers of hope to see

The galaxy, is the mind
Turning in constant motion
Freeing new thoughts and light
Throughout its limbs

Its soul, the sun
Inspiring fathomless strength
Energy, love and warmth
To every element

Of life

Union of Two

As a tranquil lake
Nourishes in silence
Growth of the lotus seed
In harmony it creates.

The lake sustains
And loves the lotus root
Fostering its growth
In freedom and in strength.

In full bloom the lotus
Beautifies the water
That helped it flower.
Inviting the hands of nature

To glorify the liquid bed
Upon which it sits
In utter comfort
Untouched by human ills.

Lured by the lotus, flitting creatures
Sow new seeds
On this pool of dreams
Remove unwanted weeds.

Growth of new life
Upon the pristine
Lake of eternity
Ensues, renewed, revived.

Such is the bond
Of lovers true
Both nourish and bloom
And in unison soar.

A New Bond

Now, I can see
Truth and love lie not in form,
They permeate deep within
Our inner core.

This Truth does live
In you, me, everything.
This Love creates all that is;
Our universe.

Don't think it wrong
Of me to long with whole heart
To walk the long road of God.
His Truth stands tall

In dark of night.
It will guide you and I to light
Take us both to lands sublime;
Soaring new heights

Above all plight.
With which we may create
A new bond of True unity:
It will not break.

Forgive me when I cannot say
What I may feel deep inside.
Sometimes words cannot explain
The glorious ways of the Divine.

True Love

True love is a union
Which breaks the bonds
Of this temporal realm
Shattering inhibitions

Of our minds and fears
When two walk as one
The world stands aside
They stride with ease through life

True love does not ask
It gives without demand
It does not look for more
Fulfilled with the one

It does not hunger
For the pleasures of many
One becomes the universe
One eternity

Its growth does not end
Even in death it lives
In the existence of
Pure seeds it thrives

To sow more words of Truth
To grow manifold
Into sweet fruit
Touching the gentle world

This love soars through us
Passed to others
Uniting all
With the realm of the infinite

Thus is love
If not thus
It is not love

Source

Love is our source
I have seen
The blood red sky
Pour, sweet crimson
Over our darkening sky
The eye
Of our growing globe
Bleeds love
To us through its life-giving
Warmth, its rays
Watch close the setting sun
As I have done
You will see endless love
Flowing
From this flowering red sphere
Ever glowing
Its jewels of light have no end
They give to us
Without fail, though we take
More than
We need to survive
Its giving
Never stops

Gulab

Red streaks as strokes
Of red paint
As veins filled with love
With life
Flow through the sky
At sunset
Pulsing through earth's eye
Reflecting upon
The great ocean
Earth's heart
Painted perfectly upon
My yearning eyes
Love is everything
Everywhere
Everyone
See the colours of earth
Hear the sounds
Touch the trees
Smell the flowers
All is love
Love is all

giaan a(n)jan bhai bha(n)janaa dhaekh nira(n) jan bhaae ||

The ointment of spiritual wisdom is the destroyer of fear; through love, the Pure One is seen.[7]

Origins

From a flowering
Abyss of love
We have come
To create enriching energy

And add to the endless flow
Of blissful light
Undying
Illuminating this earthly show

Birthing new petals pristine
Drinking rain drops
Below the tree tops
Adding to the splendour of infinity

Chapter 12

The Power of Solar

Saffron Brush

The saffron brush
Of light does touch
All things on earth
With warming love

Waking our dreams
With gentle ease
Preparing our minds
For slumbering nights

Painting our lives
With colours sublime,
All things that shine
Our earthly time

Rising Rays

The morning sun does rise
With majesty in its eyes
Dripping rays as rain
Upon mountains of air

As waterfalls of light
Diving down the laughing clouds
Forming streams entwined
With flowing rivers of gold

A site no different
Than the rainy skies
Showering mountains
With smiling streams

From the very peaks
Of great mountain tops
Sliding in steady pulse
To the great ocean's breast

The morning rise
Gently wakes the sleeping clouds
Softly brightens the nightly sky
With rays as soft as snow

These lustrous limbs of the sun
Reach beyond the blue
Beyond the clouds and birds that fly
And gently hold the earth in yellow hues

They caress our spirits
Kiss our faces and our feet
Touch every inch of our lives
Through them, the sun does speak.

Brilliant Sun

I see your rays
As they sway
They dance and play
With so much to say

Sun

Created by the warming sun
All beings share its grace
Of power, Truth and light
To give, to live, and to create

Not one of us is without the sun
Within our core it lies
Warming our heavy hearts
Through the seasons of our lives

Every eye belies the light
Of that single luminous star
Somehow it burns with splendour
Brighter with every earthly hour

Even through these cloudy days
It shines unfurling its crimson face
The grey skies of human plight
Do not taint its endless living rays

And when dark days overshadow
The joy in our searching eyes
We should seek the light deep within
Instilled in us by the sun of skies

If looking you do not find
Hope for life or healing dreams
Then look up at the livid sky
And seek that which created thee

Spectrum

Through its creation
Upon this floor
Painted subtley
In crimson hues

The sun does ask
Us to reach
Within our souls
To find our peace

To seek the Truth
Of worldly roles
Why we're here
Where we'll go

To unite in bond
In harmony
To coexist
With synergy

With every living
Earthly thing
Though diverse
To find oneness

As every colour
Of earthly site
In the spectrum
Of endless light

Sun Rise

The sun rises in the west
And it sets in the east
We have been told this since we were wee things

Born in the West, living the enlightened dream
One day I thought to travel to the Far East and see
The darkness of such unfortunate seeds

To determine how the rest survive
And in such blackness, rise
With only a setting sun before their eyes

Expecting to encounter a place dark and drear with tears
I walked in full armour and gear
With a hat on my head and boots at my heal

Well-equipped to face a battered world, in third
Full of tattered dreams and hapless words
With strange, nightly sounds unheard

A land backward and sunken
Full of people unread and drunken
A world still "developing" and unkept

Arriving on site
Ready to face the fight
I stopped in mid flight

Looking round at this novice town
I unduly, dumbfoundedly found
A place so unlike the Far East I frowned

For here was a place full of cheer
Drenched in colours not in tears
Draped in glory, not in fear

A place sprinkled with garlands of hope
Where faces were kissed by the sun with fervour
And music filled the streets with lore

Instead of dark nights I found beams of light
Brighter than any I have seen in my life
Rays of love for all those in strife

I did what in the west I never had done
I saw the rising sun more times than one
So vivid my heart sang, my soul beamed

Every morning would I wait for hours on end
To catch a glimpse of this celestial event
And hold, for a mere moment, a golden ray in my hand

I was showered, sprinkled, wrinkled
Speckled, peppered, freckled
Bewildered by the sun's power

I realised that in the east people fly
Living in the moment . . . they thrive
They have little, thus they sail above the tide

They have not wealth but have inner joy
They have not sky scrapers but have melodic lives
They have not smooth roads but have sound minds

We can learn much from this sunkist nest
To start we should know, the sun rises in the east
And it sets in the west.

Spinning Sun

Every morning the sun does rise
Calling us to look inside
And find the star that does shine
Every moment of our lives

As the sun's glow
Never does slow
Dim, darken
Or darkness allow

The sun, so great
Gently does it touch our faces
With stroking rays
Bearing warmth

"But, you say, the sun does set"
Only here, upon our earthly plain
Beyond us, light years away
It spins, ever aglow, amid starry space

Even as it sets
Within us ignites
Fire of love, passion and light
Tomorrow, again, the sun will rise

And everyday of our lives
It will shine
Amid the vast
Depths of space

With love fathomless
Somehow, the beating sun
Destinies away
Soars within my soul

Lighting days of darkness
It infuses life in my heart
Pushing me to walk
The challenging path of Earth

Sun

The sun gives more than heat,
Mere warmth and lighting waves

It exerts an energy unfound
In any Earthly element

From light years away
It emits its inner strength

Through rays instilling us
With strength, power, will

With courage, love, vigour
For us it lives; on us it pours

Unending energy of hope
Tenacity and health

Sun Set

Painted crimson skies do shine
By brushes of the saffron sun
Red, orange, yellow hues
Blended in one flawless light

My words do little justice to
Reveal the true beauty of this site serene
As though a heavenly dream pristine
A masterpiece of Truth

The sun sets in the sky
Yet rises livid within my soul
It enlightens my spirit's core
Wipes every earthly sorrow from my eyes

July 2007

Chapter 13

Lake

Let the elegant braches of the willow tree dip gently into
the still lake Wave to and fro carried by the blowing breeze,
interwined with nature's symmetry
July, 2009

Mirror

A lucid mirror of the earth,
The gentle lake reflects all life;
Upon its face, all colours birthed.
In form and shape they do arise.

Each waking night and sleeping day
The sun does set and rise with time
Observing on this liquid lake
The bright reflection of its light

Upon the darkened veil of night
Spinning among dancing pearls
Delicate lunar eyes surmise
Their Truth upon the earthly lake

These spheres of vigour and of strength
Dance in patience, never in haste
Upon the mirror embrace themselves
Within the world behold their place

As we, they too, stand curious
To see their temporal frames
Their inner beauty beaming through
The finite masks that they do wear

Knowing well, that within this plain
Of untamed pain, an endless game
Exists spirit vast and boundless
Creating all that it is—every beautiful face

Gentle Lake

In delightful radiance,
The majestic morning rays
Play with waters in harmony,
A grand, soundless symphony

Of glistening rhythmic light
Frolicking upon subtle ripples
In stance of great romance
Upon this ballroom of liquid glass.

Joining hands with each droplet blue
With precision, grace and timely form.
The rays fly, float, in grand plie
Escaping grips of earthly time.

A defiant ballet of light
Entwined in rippling melodies,
As ying and yang do merge
Unified yet unalike.

Let it not die—this ethereal dance
This song of life—this soft ballad
This display of orchestrated grace
Let the rays perform the same

Every morning on the stillness of the gentle lake

Lake

Through the fields
Of unweaved reeves
Lie seas of butterflies
Fluttering in the sunlight
Among the flocks of roses blue
Purple daffodils anew

In unison they spill
Deep into the lake
Painting it with subtle strokes
Of colours from their core
Infusing it with life blood
Flowing through nature's womb

The lake does live and breathe
As any human you may see
It bears a complexion all its own
Embedded in nature's bosom
Sharing its essence fearlessly
With all living things surrounding

Reeves

Through the fields
Of unweaved reeves
Lie seas of butterflies
Fluttering in the sunlight
Among the flocks of roses blue
Purple daffodils anew

In unison they spill
Deep into the lake
Painting it with subtle strokes
Of colors from their core
Infusing it with life blood
Flowing through nature's womb

The lake does live and breathe
As any human you may see
It bears a complexion all its own
Embedded in nature's bosom
Sharing its essence fearlessly
With all living things surrounding

Chapter 14

Dear Forest—Our True Wealth

Forest

Walking through the forest green
I found great wisdom lie
Among the drying wilted leaves
Climbing high the ivy vines

I saw peace in forest's every limb
Entwined within spider's web
Entrenched in great cedar's skin
Carried so in acorn's breast

Tall trees of earthen branch
Of rugged flesh, hardened bark
I saw them rooted deep in land
Fairing all weathers beneath the stars

Fearless trees unnerved
By upheavels here surrounding
I saw them lending hands
To every living being

I found the way through "pathless woods"
To a lake of timeless voice
Whistling songs of soundless Truth
Adorned with gentle lotus wings

This lake I found lied nowhere else
But deep within this human flesh
Beneath all the eyes can sense
Beyond the veils of form and earth
    The forest led me abound

Sheltered from noise and drear
Safe from stares unsound
Away from every fear

As a cool whispering breeze
I felt the emerald forest breathe
And with its every release
It did stir the lotus lake in me

Lying deep within
Connecting all that is
With eternal words
Carrying universal Truth

We are one—Ek Ong Kaar

Temple

Every tree is a temple
Tall and wise
Forest green
Holding all in its place
With gentle grace

Shading young and old
Flower and stone
From sun and rain
Hail, sleet and snow

Reaching the heavens
Speaking to the skies
A home to all
Birds, bees, flies

Each year growing larger
With more to attend
In season bearing fruit
For anyone's delight

With roots of gold
Reaching into wisdom untold
Expansive and vast
Knowledge, understanding, bliss and stillness

Rain drops, dew from its tears
Each ray of light its shining smile
Every delicate flower
An expression of the Creator

Earth's gift to all who see
Its offering of love and peace
Nature lives and breathes
As you and me

It too needs to be free
Grow in harmony
To deny it life
Is to deny ourselves

Uganda, 2010

To bind and shackle it
Is unjust
Let the elegant branches
Of the Willow tree dance

Into the still lake; Wave to and fro carried
By the breeze Intertwined with nature's symmetry
Every tree is a temple
Each stream a flowing field of dreams
Every hill sprinkled with mystery

All plants worlds of wealth
The mountain a fountain of strength
Grass carpets of pristine green
Stones, stories of old earth's bones

Fallen leaves strands of earth's hair
The soil, earth's warm flesh
The lakes its' lucid eyes
Running rivers its' arteries keeping Earth alive

The great ocean its' heart and soul
From this all things abound
Each gentle breeze and heavy wind its' breath
Every dessert and sand bed it soft cheeks

Shaped and formed by the shifting winds
Every tree is a temple
Shelter for those alone
Shade for the alone, the unknown
Never will they be forgotten

Knowledge and wisdom
Resonates within every branch
With the tempests and eternal beat
Of our sacred source

As the Holy cross
The feather of the eagle
The wheel of Buddha
The moon of Islam
The star of Davide
The Khanda of Sikhi

Every leaf flies, soars
And stands as a symbol of infinity
Teaching with every intake
Of our polluted air

Inhaling toxins only to provide us fresh air
And to grant us life upon this path of earth
Our sight, strength and wisdom
Is a gift from the pristine nature around us

Every tree is a temple
The breath of life

Tree

One calm day
I did see
A tall tree hold
The world in its embrace

It stretched high
Into the blue
Sullen skies
Against their pale hues

Somehow it stood
Taller than all
Things created
By the sprawling

Human race

Divine branch

A branch
Of the Divine tree
I live and breathe
Still, I last

I am a part
Of all that is
One vessel
Of the universal heart

We are all, we are
The great light, infinity
We are the creative source
We are none other than
 Love
 Harmony
 Peace
 Creation
 Truth

We are all God

Arbutus Tree, 2006

Forest Tall

I stood with the forest tall
Looked beyond the forest walls

Searched within forest bark
For Truth, meaning, life and love

From within me I did call
And asked great forest for answers all

"Trees of peace at your feet I fall
Inspired by your wordless wonder

Your majestic walls
Do save me in the dark of night

From the plight of pitiful
Human woes, these human cries

Your painted greens and playful paths
Dance before my yearning eyes."

"Yes," you say, "there is a way
To escape confusion of human wrath

There is a Truth and a new day,
See the silent script upon my walls

Here exists no fear and no dismay
No desire, no anger, no empty calls

Here, we live in peace and joy
Despite the state of the external

Think only of the eternal

Ek ong kaar
Sat Naam
Karta Purakh
Nirbhau Nirvair
Akaal Murat
Ajuni Saibangh."

Sacred trees in you I see
The vibrant light of infinity

Chapter 15

Nature's Verse

We Belong to Earth

The Earth cannot be shackled and bought
By a few crisp bank notes numbered by human hands
Worth nothing in eternity, in our grand universe
Earth is an entity, unbounded in our majestic galaxy
As liberated and free as we

So much of our Earth has been altered and torn
Damaged and soiled
A patchwork of concrete jungles
Human consumption, artificial wealth
Upon lands not meant to be altered

This landscape has raised us
Providing us with all we need
To grow and flourish
Yet, for the things that will never fulfill us
The Earth is depleted and our hunger only grows.

Within us
Dwells Love that is free and true, *priceless*
It is all that can and ever could
Fulfill our beings
Love is more precious than wealth, *it is why we are here. Nothing more.*

Dear Earth

The earth dies, for it does not belong to us.
We belong to it. Yet, we believe it is ours to own.
We have destroyed so much of our pristine home
As the patchwork of human communities and concrete
jungles grow.

So does the need for the artificial and material grow within
us
The more our need for materiality and consumer goods
increases,
The Earth is sought to fulfill this void.
The ocean of clouds flows through the deep valleys of
mountainous peaks

As streams and rivers, the canals of clouds rush in stillness
through the
Bright mountains of light
The clouds as heavenly waters fly
Through layers of air and rugged, sublime Earth.

As frosted plains of snow the clouds do glow
Inviting us to imagine and dream of possibilities yet
beyond human thought
There is a way to master this paradise of perfection upon
our earthly plains
A way to sustain, to save our world without compromise.

There is a way for us to go beyond sky scrapers and build
sky sustainers
Enmeshed in the world
Dwellings where we may live and thrive,
Fly and touch the skies.

Abodes where we are immersed in the majestic land
Where it is enriched by our growth
Not depleted by our consumption
Sustainable worlds infinitely harmonious with nature—
that we are an integral part of.

We may create or destroy that which feeds us and gives us life,
To which we belong.
For it is this Earth, and nothing else,
That gives life to our children, and that has given life to our ancestors
It has birthed our past, present and future.

It is our gentle world that bears every fruit and every space fit for our lives.
It is our gentle Earth upon which our utter existence depends, and the existence
Of everything that lives depends.
Without Earth, we will no longer be.

Sculpted Earth

Sculpted mounds of Earth
Each piece perfectly chiselled and perfected
Each inch a part of a grand artistic display
Our Earth remains the cosmic gem of our galaxy.

To create on land and sea as in the air
Stars for abodes and Earth to work,
Farms revealing the essence of diversity
Not bounded monotony

A perfect harmony and peace as the sky
So our Earth can be.

Mountain Range

Forests of mountains do rest upon the land
Each range an intricate display,
Revealing patterns as leaves and trees

Rare Earth

The ocean of clouds flows through the
Deep valleys of mountainous peaks

As streams and rivers, the canals of clouds rush
In stillness through the bright mountains of light.

The clouds as heavenly waters fly
Through the air and rugged, sublime earth

As frosted plains of snow, the clouds do glow
Inviting us to imagine and dream of possibilities
beyond human thought

There is a way to master this paradise
Of perfection upon our earthly plains

Upon the branches of mountain ranges
And the hills and valleys shaped as leaves upon earth

A way to sustain, to save our world without compromise
There is a way for us to go beyond sky scrapers

And build instead that which sustains our lands
Dwelling where we may live and thrive, fly and touch
the skies

Abodes where we are immersed in the majestic land,
Where it is enriched by our growth not depleted by
consumption

Sustainable worlds of infinite harmony
With nature that we are an integral part of

We may create or destroy that which gives us life
The land to which we belong

For it is this Earth, and nothing else,
That gives life to us, our children, our ancestors, our
past, present and future

It is our gentle world that bears every
Fruit and every space fit for our lives.

It is our rare earth upon which our utter existence
And the existence of everything that lives depends.

Without Earth we will no longer be.
Love Earth and let it grow within thee.

The Cure for Cancer

The ocean is the sky and the sky is the land
As the evaporation and condensation
Result in the oceans vaporization to the skies
The skies rejoin the land through rain
Raining upon us and upon the Earth
Watering our fields,
Our crops and our dinner plates

The toxins in our oceans, oil spills and chemical spills
Sewage we eat in our fruits and vegetables, cheese and meat.
We eat that which we spill
Into our vast oceans, lakes and seas

We eat toxins, oil, waste, rust and rubbish,
The cure for cancer is ultimately

The end of oil transport upon our waters.

An end to polluting and littering in our oceans.

It is a choice and a commitment we must make.

Spirit

Light of our spirit's core
Lingers within our heart's door
In constant brilliance
As the sun's subtle dance

Unchanging, untainted
Unwavering, untouched
A pure abyss, fathomless
Vast, enduring, endless

This timeless light revealed
And its glory unleashed
Frees what lies deep within
And to the world it sings

As the newly formed wings
And tender, gentle limbs
Delicate and swift
Transformed within the chrysalis

Of the radiant butterfly.
Such metamorphosis of life
From a thing that crawls,
To one that flies above all.

Transformed, we too will fly
With wistful wings to glide
Us beyond the burdening weight
Of a cumbersome human fait

To a place of peace
Of limitless light and ease
With poverty a nightmare
Forgotten and erased.

From the canvas of the earth.

Soar

As the sun shines brighter
On a clear, cloudless sky
With few stoic shadows
Its brightness knows no bounds.

So too, our inner sun,
The light within us
Releases bright beams
When we are freed from fear

Soar through the skies
With your wings to new heights
Release your rays
Not tomorrow, today

Light

In the absence of your light my Lord
I am a tree without roots
A lamp without light
A flower unbloomed

I am a body without life
A heart without pulse
A canyon without depth
A bird with no wings

Without your love my Lord
I am a lake with no water
A sky without clouds
A face with no smile

Music with no sound
Eyes without dreams
A soul intoxicated
With unsound fears

An unsteady sea
A mind corrupted
A day without sun
The Night with no moon

With your pure light my Sweet Lord
I am a star shining bright
A brilliant ray of light
A heart full of might

I have eyes with clear sight
I am free
To see reality
To know and to lead

All people to simplicity
I can glide, I can soar
As a lion I can roar
Open new possibilities, new doors

Walk paths to peace, ending all wars.

Chapter 16

Mist

Fog

Through the thickest fogs
The heaviest rains
The stormiest days
And heedless loss

Shoot rays of gold
From the pocket of wealth
The soul of strength
The star of hope

The sun will rise
After every night
The storms subside
As gentle light
Pours through the sky

Formless

The morning mist
Thus rises from
The gentle lake
All days of sun

Mist is not mist
Look deep, look in
Mist is not one
Many is mist

Mist is us
You me and all
Dancing droplets
Of pure water

Dancing as sprites
Upon its face
Flying away
Back to the sky

But as they fly
These droplets shine
Waltzing with light
A majestic site

Not knowing if they
Should stay immersed
In the grand lake
Or reunite above

Oh lake,
If I could be
A droplet as free
As those caressing
Your gentle waves

I too would dance
Upon your stage
Of watery blue
Clear as glass

I too would bathe
In morning light
Be carried away
By warming rays

And find a place
Above the blue
Without form or hue
Among the air

Thick Mist

Through the thickest of mists
And thickest of fogs
Stand light rays released
From the star of hope

The sun's rays as breath
Warm our world, our hearts
Even on darkening days
Filled with stormy rain

The sun speaks volumes
Listen, feel, and watch
Its subtlety, its touch
See and never be lost

As humanity, each day, every year, nature grows and blooms with more vibrance and vivacity than the year before. In Spring the blossoms reveal new branches that have stretched far into the sky in every direction. No branch is without blossoms. Each Spring, new buds are formed. This is the way of every wondrous natural creation. Nature lives without boundaries or confinement . . . in liberty it thrives. The ways of nature are sublime and astounding. They cannot be replicated by any earthly form. They just are.

In comparison, the world created by humans is often concrete and square. Enclosed in an unending maze of walls, boundaries, sign post, demands, and fences. Who are we hiding from? Who are we turning away? These boundaries close us off from ourselves more than any perceived enemy or outside threat. The walls we have put up around our lives also bar us from entering our own inner worlds. The less we open ourselves up to all people and all creatures of the earth, the less we understand who we are. The more we lose ourselves in shallow pursuits such as, addiction and materialism.

The homes, buildings, and shops created by humans do not grow and bloom each year but age, wither and decay. The human world is enclosed to such an extent that it attempts to confine nature in its boundaries as well. The trees are cut down or trimmed for wider streets, bigger homes or power lines. Nature is placed in particular order based on what humans consider aesthetically pleasing. City streets are decorated with trees. In doing so, humans have disrupted nature's natural cycle of life. In turn, the livelihood and survival of all life on Earth is now at risk. All creatures are fundamentally connected to nature. Every living being is made up of earth, water, wind, fire. Yet, the human world has and is continually dividing itself from nature and dividing nature from itself—from that which sustains all existence on Earth.

Chapter 17

The Power of Peace

Peace

When all is at peace
Quiet with ease
Nature in harmony
In silence softly speaks

Through the noise of the world
Clamour, uproars, and wars
One cannot quite see
Nor hear Truth . . . so near

It won't be found
On bloody grounds
Of battered souls
Fighting for the freedom

They shackle and tear

Or in fields of uprooted and rotting trees
Hunted flesh of great species
In the diamond mines filled with young hands
Picking pieces of gold for temporary glamour

No, it does not exist,
In hatred and envy
Lust, pride and desire
In patience it lies

I have searched
The wide world
For this Truth

Its tender roots

Little I found
When in dispair
I wined, pined and cried
I was lost and I died

When my searching stopped
Quiet were my thoughts
Life pointed me within
There it stood good and still

Deep within my spirit
Permeating my soul
Lied the answers I sought
A literature untold

The jewels were within
Though I sought them out there
In the clouds and the rain
Here, within me they reigned

When we quiet our minds
Our fears and petty cries
Gentle, wordless Truth
With sweet ways, does sooth

Teaching us to live and soar
As the lotus and the swan
Above the waves of worldly woes
Exuding beauty for all to behold.
Not in War.

Journey

I journey the wild world and behold
Towering forests of evergreen
Bordered by fresh rivers of gold
Under the glowing sun pristine
Veiled at eve with moonlit haze
Where only stars and waters shine

Beyond these brows I discover
Scented, floral paths of red earth
Enjeweled by sweet coconut groves
Of palm trees bearing fruit of milk
Spilling into hills and valleys of carved stones
Chiseled as sculptures of the seasons

I travel further along jaws
Of treasured greenery
Upon the coast, castles of flawless rock
Where the air is thick with heat
And the land abundant with fruit
Ripe with all shades of the spectrum

Bordering soft eyes of deep blue
Waving in and out to shore
Upon them colours bloom
Reflections of the surrounding stones
Soft majenta and purple hues
Watching in silence the warring world

Though bearing different complexions
All features of earth, brushed by the sun
And bathed by the silver moon, are one
Venturing east, west, south and north
I view one earthly visage
Immaculate with beauty and worth

Life of light, earth, water, and air,
Upon the adorned face of earth,
Is moulded from a single clay
In the eyes of worldly beings
I see one purpose, one ache
To live in love, in joy, in peace.

**Varan bhaekh asaroop eaeko eaeko
sabadh viddaanee[8]**

Colour, dress and form were contained in the One
Lord; the shabad was contained in the one
wondrous Lord.

Life, a breath, in the heart of eternity.

A blink in the eyes of the universe

Nature's company,
In quiet harmony,
A subtle ambience, reveals,
The glory of creation.

Time

Nature has depths of time
Unfathomed by the human eye

Layers of life unseen, unswept
And thus untouched by human plight

A Truth so deep, so out of reach
It can only be experienced not seen

An intricacy so beyond our capabilities
It cannot be recreated by humanity

A network so vast, so efficient
We cannot behold its essence

Our refusal to see Nature's true face
Has caused us to undervalue its place

We have placed it below ourselves
In the web of life we create

We have bound nature in shackles
It is slave to our needs

We have destroyed its harmony
Exploiting it for our own faculties

Thinking this borrowed land stands
Solely for our hands.

Chapter 18

The Power of the Living Ocean

70% of our Earth consists of oceans. They connect the lands of our world together. Unfortunately, we enjoy a variety of amenities and conveniences often at the expense of our oceans. Most countries in our world depend on the ocean transport of oil and other harmful fossil fuels to provide energy for various daily activities such as, driving, lighting, heating, cooling systems, cooking and water heating systems. Oil transport has proven to be a great detriment to our oceans and its living species. And we cannot reverse the damage caused by oil spills. Oil lingers in our most important and abundant natural resource for millennia. Still, more countries such as America and parts of South America continue to construct new oil drilling sites that have a risk of further oceanic contamination. The contamination of the ocean inevitably leads to toxins in our agricultural lands, fish and rain water. As a technological innovation to prevent oil spills, Brazil has been a leader in natural ethanol production from sugar cane by-products that do not contaminate the environment. Instead of chasing profits from oil drilling, we need to promote such innovation and research in solar and battery powered cars or non-polluting oil sources.

Rise and Fall

The hills and valleys
Of the livid silver brine
Sway in constant rhythmic motion and unwind
Travelling in fine balance toward brilliant sites

Until a single wave soars to unseen heights touching the
sun sublime
Leaving far below the deep emerald brine.
Licked by the majestic sun's glare divine
It basks in the glory of luminescent pride.

In time, the passing breeze eases its reign with simple
stride
Whisking it below the sea, "bereaving it of light"
Whispering sea winds then clear for the rise
Of a new oceanic crest to shine in the sunlit sky

As the melodic sway of the waves, our lives
See rise and fall throughout the winds of time.
Testing our mettle, our might,
Our destiny soars then sinks in our mind's eye

We move together as the liquid brine
One great ocean of fleshed light
Inhaling, exhaling the breath of our destiny
Glory and misery befalling all in line

In glory climbing untouched heights
We share our light with passing lives
Revealing the pleasure of soaring so high
Too high to be seen by envious eyes

Our test, to smile,
Through not only day,
But pitiful night,
Is the test of time.

Inspired by the collective meditation and chanting of spiritual song in a place of worship. The sangat was as an ocean of bliss chanting in unison, as the waves of the ocean roar—a great symphony.

Ocean

As the ocean breathes
So do we
Inhaling deeply air full of life
Releasing energy in time
The waves rolling
Upon each breath

So too,
Living beings do
Take in the world
The air unfolds
Within our mould

Giving life to our bones
And strength for us to grow
The inner vibration
Continues within the heart
As the breath of life
Within us soars

-2010, bus from Mbarara to Kampala

Symphony

Stirring the deep blue melody
As a violin soft and sweet
Creatures of the sea do sing
And dance and rhyme in harmony

A grand symphony under the sea
All parts creating tones their own
In this ballad of subtlety
Not a note is lost to the unknown

The sand beneath whisped by the waves
Births seaweed to sway, laugh and play
Amidst the coral, a stage of grand display
On this oceanic stage miracles are made.

Lite

As the waves of the salty brine
Reach unseen heights
And the full moon on a cloudless night
Reveals its luminous face with glorious ease.

So too, the beauty of our spherical souls shines
Illumines our very heart with destined time
Shedding Truth in the dark of night
As it walks towards universal light.

Chapter 19

The Power of the Wind

After observing the moon veiled by patterned clouds in late evening—a celestial site. I stepped out of my car and transfixed my eyes upon the lunar display adorning the sky. Although it was so high above me, I felt as though I was part of it. The moon watched me as I watched it.

Vancouver, October 2007

Velvet Sky

Travelling through the velvet sky
Of silver, shimmering, snowy hues
The clouds in union crest the night
Appearing as though untouched dunes
Of pearl white sands in distant lands
Streaked subtley with lunar hands

Sailing, an island in the sky
Surrounded by oceans of air
Rippling through darkened, royal heights
As the airy sea frees its breast
Releasing the tide from its grains
To reveal pristine art of its waves

This sandy beach, these dunes do fly
Far above our mountain peaks
Studded with silent, shining stars
As if a scene from the Earth freed
Into the sky to remind us
Who we are and from where we've come

In rhythmic motion with quiet ease
Blown by the wind's endless breath
The clouds swim through the starry seas
To find their True destination
They move in flocks, in herds, in armies
Endless, in perfect harmony

Bowing in humble stance as they pass
The wondrous face of the moon
The clouds are blessed by her brow
And continue to glide through the blue
Beneath the stars, above the trees,
Carressed by the gentle eve.

Winds of Spring

The winds of Spring
Sing as they swing
From leaf to skin
From wave to mist

Blowing past everything
Bringing forth rings
Of pink blossom trees
Unseen, seldom heard, winds of spring

Sweet seeds fly and unwind
In the womb of time
To be planted and to rise
On windy wings to fly

Unleashed by the winds of Spring.

Winds

The whispering winds
Do ask
The Autumn leaves
To Fall
In honour of the coming frost
To free
The branches for snowy flakes
To rest.
In a moment of peace
Leaves die
Leaving their mothering branches
As do all
Beings of life
To lie
One with the moistened Earth
And drink
The dew drops of grey clouds
In time
Nourish the roots which created them
In symbiosis
Live the elements of nature
In death
Giving life to new green
In life
Giving air for us to breathe.

Winds of Hope

The winds of hope
Do brush our cheeks
When days are cold
Our hearts feel weak

They hold our hands
Hug our sleeves
Remind us that
Peace is near

The winds of hope
Kiss our heads
When we are down
They laugh and play

They wake us up
When we're asleep
Pull us out of
Sorrow's way

The winds of hope
Tap our windows
When we are lost
They open new doors

Listen for them
Feel them, see them
Near or far
They're here, everywhere

The Winds of Hope

Clouds

Flying high
Above the cloudy sky
My eyes surmise
A snowy site

As arctic fields of ice
Stretching far beyond our plight
The clouds at the peak of the sky lie
Untouched plains of snowy light

Inviting me to lie
Upon their lofty heights
And create with ease and delight
An imprint of my site

Cloudy Night

As the sun on a cloudy day
And the waves upon a calm sea

The wind on a still day
And the Earth under cement streets

When the moon starts a new phase
As the lotus lies below the stream

And tulips under Autumn leaves
Growing green beneath cement streets

The rain on a cloudless day
And ice in the summer sun

Human souls found astray
On roads thick with dismay

Will enlighten in due time
Shadowed by worldly dreams

Sand Dunes

Sand dunes do sit in sunny streams
Of golden rays swimming quickly by
Thus creviced with every beam
Of soft light poured from gleaming skies

An orange world of sandy grains
Sprinkled with lustrous sunny drops
Radiating the desert face
Not a speck of rain is seen to stop

Upon this sandy smile pristine
The dunes do dance with light
Swept by the beat of the warming breeze
Leaving the liquid world behind

Freedom

Freedom is the essence of the universe.
It is integral to joy and to progression.

Freedom is the way of nature.
Freedom is the law of existence.

Free are the sun and its rays,
To reach through space.

Free is the water,
To travel any place.

Free is the earth,
To grow and to erode.

Free are the winds
To dance through time.

Free are the trees
To laugh and play.

So, tell me why it is
Humans are not free?

On the creation of a painting made only by the colours of elements in nature such as leaves, grass, flower petals, earth, roots, branches, and fruit.

Colours

The colours of nature
Bleed upon the page
Their love, their light, their worth
What they bear within they display

Wind

When all is calm and at peace
And we least expect the breeze

The playful wind does carress
The maple trees with Autumn scents

As our fathers tickle our toes
Grab our ears and hug our souls

The winds do tickle the trees
Shaking and waking their leaves

As if the wind can see how
And when the trees are lying low

Sending a gust of wind to dash
And lift the branches smooth and fast

The trees do rejoice at the feel
Of their friends who lie so near

Laughing and playing in cheer
With this ancient love of years

The trees do know to the wind they owe
The spread of their kind, new and old

Without the winds, trees could not free
Their seeds to sprout in fruitful fields

Paint this livid earthly scene
With leaves of red, yellow and green

Colouring the world anew, every season
Eventually to fly again with the wind

U.S. October 2007

Dark Night

In the dark of night
Bright stands the light

Speaking alone, a single spark
In the midst of the false

Within pain their is pleasure
Searching for True treasure

Shining all the brighter
When seen in ill weathers

In sickness there is strength
To survive and regain health

In heartache their is realization
Of the nature of Love

Blushing Clouds

Upon the arrival
Of the morning sun
The clouds do blush
Colouring the earthly face
With soft shades of rouge
Glowing in joy at growing rays

Sky

The subtle winds, in the laughing sky
Soar, dance, sing, swirl, among all
Writing verse as nature's loyal scribe
Drawing signs on our silent walls

Upon a thick layer of clouds
They tell tales for us to read
Messages changing form
With every movement on this green

Great essays of Truth and time
In symbols, shapes and streaks
Read these lines sublime
 Turn the pages of destiny

The more you search for answers
For Truth of purpose and essence of life
You will see that which is always present
Nature's verse, on every path in site

Chapter 20

Universe

The entire universe speaks. The trees, the sky, the seas, the leaves, the sun, the moon, and the soil—the earth, the fire, the wind, the rain, the birds, and the breeze do speak. The eagle, the hawk, and the raven whisper Truths. They tell us to soar higher . . . above the chaos of the human world. They guide our way. The world tells us there is more. It speaks of what was, what is, what will be.

Stop . . . quiet your mind . . . look and listen; hear, see, smell, feel, taste the messages. Everyday the earth speaks through its sky, the sun, the clouds, the lakes and all living creatures. We do not hear it because we are consumed, engulfed in our own worldly lives, our trivial thoughts. If we could clear, dissolute our minds and meditate on the universe, we would hear Truth. Every question is answered, every sorrow dispelled, every story told, every desire met. Quiet your mind . . . . hear the Truth.

Nebula

As the majestic wombs of light
Amid the pristine veils of space
Beyond all human site
Clouds of gold join to create
Brilliant stars which light the skies

So too, a woman's womb in time
Gives life to seeds of universal light
With love and peace helps them rise
To grow within this dream and shine
Brilliant sparks of Truth to ease human plight

Infinitude

The eye of infinity,
A site serene,
An endless reality
Filled with Truth unseen

Peacock Feather

The feather of a peacock
Is more inspiring
In all its intracacies
And complexities of colour
A universal masterpiece
In all of its detail
Its soft beauty, a true glory
Its humble texture,
Holding a beauty unknowing
Not a thing we make
On this earthly plain
Will ever compare

Scribe

As nature speaks
So I write
What I hear
I speak
What I see
I set free

Chapter 21

Earth

Gentle Earth

The gentle earth gives birth
To all colours on this plain
Which swim like fish or fly like birds
Through shades of Autumn days

It listens to soft songs
Of robins in the spring
And the solemn stones
Speak of common things

It sees the waters rise
Frees the falling tide
Shimmer in ambient lights
Aglow in moonlit nights

Earth smiles at their gaiety
As the children run and play
It feels their tender feet
Upon its gentle face
The earth whistles with the wind
And cries with the rain
It radiates with the sun
And crashes with the waves
So let us dance and play
Eat, share and pray
Laugh and sing the days away
For the gentle earth is here to stay

Young Earth

As a vibrant, playful child
The earth dances in the lap
Of the beaming sun
Spinning throughout its days.

The smiling sun sustains
This young earth of blue and green
Easing every pain
Feeding every hungry limb.

It warms earth's gentle seas
With sweet rays of shining gold
Bathing from east to west
Its rugged yet tender flesh.

And livens the blushing skies
With bright, blossomed light
Changing with every site
At day pale blue and rouge by night

The sun brushes its utter breath
Instilling such warmth and life
As that found deep within,
Deep within you and I.

Artful Tales of Earth

In silence the earth does sit,
Upon this starry wonder
This dark plain of opulence,
Observing its endless splendour

The bright moon within her grasp
Lamps the sunless nights
For souls who've lost their way
To safely tread paths of light

Day and night the earth does watch
Beings of all shades take flight
And listens with care
Their stories of joy, sorrow, humour and fright

Sung and said, written and painted
Upon this grand stage of games
By figures young and aged
Of what they've seen throughout their days

Stories of life, of travel and fun
Stories of who they are what they feel
Stories of dreams they will fulfill
Stories of ancient scripts, and deeds

Spring

As Spring blossoms in the breeze,
Blowing freely through earth and sea
Landing with gentle ease
Where the wind decides to cease

When they have bloomed and graced
Their tender birth place
The trees from which they came
They leave their nests and sale

They fly to distant shores
Above the rocky coves
Floral walks, grassy groves
And call this new place home

Some soar through the skies awhile
Until they touch watery beds
Upon which they float and lie
Basking under sunny rays,

As Spring blossoms in the breeze
We, too, grow in such harmony
Touch all those around with energy
Every Spring our spirits are freed

Spring

Written on a day when I faced ill weathers and heartache. I felt a great pain and a sense of hopelessness due to a negative experience. I began to give up on life and saw no way, no path, no hope. After a few minutes of crying in my car, I noticed the sun begin to shine. Not long after, I noticed a great eagle soaring above me. I got out of my car and looked up. It was flying in a sacred circle high in the sky. My crying subsided and, somehow, I was filled with feelings of hope and inspiration.

Eagle

With grace and ease
Solemn, steady sway
The great eagle makes its way
Through cool, crisp breeze

It fairs all weathers
Under the sun
All weathers as one
One too, with itself

It seeks not praise
Not approval
From the temporal
With the formless it sales

Its utter being
Fierce in peace
Alone yet vast
Unconquered, undying

The eagle is an image
Of hope prospering
Vision unending
Expansive reach

The eagle is strength
In utter weakness.
It soars relentless
In sinking worlds.

In flight it waltzes
With playful winds
In perfect motion
Silent harmony

Its black wings,
Gentle as petals
Strong and steady,
Say to us all, "persevere"
In your time of need,
Grasped unprepared
By life's bitter winds,
Seek the strength of the eagle's way—

It's grace, its flight, it's strength, its being
Is intertwined with the light of the Infinite Spirit

Soar

As a single eagle soars

Gliding gently in grace

It reaches the heights of the sky

Inspiring all who cast their eye

The eagle, master of the clouds,

Allowing it to fly with ease

And with patience

Let me too become an eagle

Flying to the pinnacles

Of human thought

And potential

Globe

Birds of unity
    Sing melodically
        With the kind winds
            And every earthly thing

The trees live free
    From all hatred and fear
        From guilt and drear
            Alligned with all that is

The coming winds
    Carress every thing
        Spreading their worth
            Upon all hearts of earth

We too will shine
    When we see all in one
        And, in one, all
            When all rise, and not one falls

We too will fly
    When, with quiet minds,
        We find inner light
            And see the Truth of life

When all souls enjoy
            Love
                harmony
                    peace

We will find
    Pristine paradise

The Eagle Soars Above

The eagles soar above me
Asking me to dream

The eagles soar above me
And I am released

The eagles soar above me
Have no fear

The eagles soar above me
And peace is near

The eagles soar above me
And I am freed

The eagles soar above me
The way is clear

City Streets

Amidst the noise and the strain
Of chaotic busy city lanes
The many voices of human play
Driving through our rushing veins

The traffic on concrete roads
Mimicking our rushing thoughts
Travelling in combustion on and on
Through our windy mindful folds

Laden amidst this play of form
This circus of floating words
Pockets of silence lie alone
Unwavered by woeful worlds

Nature sits unstirred
As a motionless mime,
Among crowds of cries
Shouting, stewing, sobbing,

In complete poise and stillness it lies
Surrounded by a world chasing time
As if it sees a light
A quiet way out of fleshed plight

A path to creative harmony
Where all life is full and free
Shackles of order have no place
Existence of the highest symmetry

Now

What have we done,
Where are we now
So far from home
Our ethereal throne

What was once true
Our essence, our hue
muddied by dreams
As is around us so is
Within us—polluted seas

God is Light

God
Is a force
Translucent
A power
Discernible
A flower
Untouchable
A fire
Unbeatable
A light
Our universal source
Which creates
From darkness
Manifests
In all things
Yet can be
Held
Touched
Captured
Altered
Tainted
By nothing
Light is life
Light is God

On the 16th Floor

I do believe that there is a realm beyond this
Within which abides a society absorbed in truth
Somehow intertwined with the starry cosmos
Enlightened by the wisdom of the Supreme Guru

Even as I sit here,
On the 16th floor of a tall square building, in a bland square office
With only a computer screen and a mahogany door to view
I feel something deep within my spirit
Telling me there is more

Somehow there exists within my heart
A surety that there is a greater reality
Where unfathomed beauty does exist
A spiritual consciousness illuminated by eternal celestial music.

Untouched by the woes of the human world

-10/15/2004

Ants

I sit observing silent, fastidious ants crawl about the
concrete floor
Wondering where they come from . . . where they go
Wondering where my destiny begins . . . where it ends
Thinking about the purpose of my life . . . our lives

Why do we wander about and work busily in this world?
Investing so much strength and thought to create that
which is temporary
Why do we consume ourselves with worldly events
Like ants who toil over food and abode on this concrete
floor?

Perplexed and unsettled I leave the ants to their work.

Walking inside shop doors I notice 3 flags hanging from
the ceiling

The answer to my questions perhaps?

Perhaps.

"Love, peace and harmony."
"Love, peace and harmony."
The words upon the flags
Whisper to me like Apparitions in Shakespeare's <u>Macbeth</u>

I am enlightened.
We exist, we struggle, we wander
To achieve . . . love, peace and harmony
Within ourselves . . . with one another

Perhaps life is simpler than we think

July, 2005

Puzzle

Years we spend
Composing the pieces of our lives
Placing them together in perfect alignment
Fitting our days together like the pieces of a puzzle

So intricate
Yet so complicated
We make the web of our life

If we could take it apart
What would we find beneath our quilted lives?

Simplicity of Existence . . . One universal Light.

Mosaic

An intricate mosaic
Of colour we are,
A delicate work of art
We are a colourful mosaic

Each piece has its place
In this grand tapestry
Where it sits
Until placed somewhere new

Each part a masterpiece
Has a true beauty its own,
Each piece
Has a wonder beyond words of praise

The more contrasting
The brighter
more vibrant they seem
Bright as a peacock's feathers they gleam

No one is black, no one white
We are one, we *are*
One mosoaic of light
One grand majestic mosaic of light

Freedom

We are free
In our land
To live and be
Our best

We are free
On this plain
To achieve
That which we demand

We are free
To breathe
Air produced by any tree
Emerging from beneath

We are free
To roam
As we please
To any place, together or alone

We are free
To swim
In every lake, river, sea
Delve deep into earth's lucid skin

We are free
To climb
Earth's unfathomed peaks
And behold the land from a bird's eye

We are free
To soar, to glide, to fly
Feel the sweet breeze
Of earth's brilliant skies

We are free.
But what of those earthly beings
Living in captivity
Unable to roam, swim, soar, where they need?

As we, they deserve liberty
To cherish every element of harmony
Intrinsic to this universal body
And walk upon any path to fulfill their empyreal destiny

Masterpiece

I have seen the mould of the Earth
Its delicate shapes,
Wondrous life
Endless gifts.

I have seen the mountains rest upon the sky
While blushing light Exude shades of mauve and rouge
In the twilight

I have adored the swaying waves
Flowing gracefully to the whispering winds
A site sublime, so majestic and vast, I could cherish it for
eternity

I have gazed upon the stars, in the midnight hours, carrying
hope, faith and Truth from the Heavens. Telling in a subtle
way to carry on, carry on the torch of life on Earth.

I have seen the sea, a masterpiece unmatched by any other
form. The Earth a grand creation, put together as a puzzle
against the crashing waves. The sky a work of indescribable
beauty, embellishing every breath of life.

The sun, an immaculate creation, birthing all that is upon
our Earth.

And all that is...

A masterpiece, more inspiring and majestic than any creation in our galaxy.

Each day we walk upon this masterpiece,

A pristine work of art, a paradise of life...

To sustain it.

Afterword

In order for India to reach a level of universal electrical capacity, it must unify and select one objective plan of action which is followed by all states. It would be beneficial for all states to follow a strategic plan in order to fulfill the goals of the JNNSM under the guidelines and supervision of one ministry review board. In China, for instance, over 98% of households have electricity, not because of a higher GDP, but because of efficient measures of strategic project implementation. Cooperating and working together to pool resources will increase time and efficiency. Central resource support and administration can be filtered through the National Solar Mission financed through IREDA or another administrative wing for rural electrification.

India has limitless potential in solar, wind, hydro and biomass energy yet it has not fully accessed its potential in renewable energy as other states. In Brazil, for instance, 80% of the energy is derived from hydro-power. Brazil also has the most sophisticated bio-fuel supply system in the world. President Luiz Inácio Lula da Silva of Brazil stepped into a plummeting economy and increased economic productivity by providing a $150.00 stipend to all slum dwellers and people of lower-socio economic backgrounds who sent their children to school and provided them with health care. This helped to close social divides and build a larger middle class that was investing in the economy by purchasing large appliances. All states with a large slum population would highly benefit from monthly stipends. Through collective efforts for policy change India may enable underprivileged people to invest in their future and attain energy access, increasing their health security and human development levels.

In 2010, Pavan started the Lotus Foundation for Children to help build shelters and primary schools for families in rural low socio-economic areas with minimal energy access.

Gurpavan continues to work with the Society for Deprived Classes Education and Fielding Nair Architect, Suhasini Ayer to build a Primary school in Ambavaram Village, India.

For more information please contact:

The Lotus Foundation for Children
P.O. Box 60089 RPO
Fraser St.
Vancouver, BC
V5W 4B5
604-671-0851
http://thelotusfoundationforchildren.blogspot.ca/

References

AGECC. (2010). Energy for a Sustainable Future: Summary Report and Recommendations. United Nations. Pg. 2-24.

Alienation of Tribal and Daliths Lands Committee on State Agrarian Relations and Unfinished Task of Land Reforms: Chapter Four. (2009). Ministry of Rural Development, Government of India. Retrieved July 22, 2010 from http://vishalmishra.com/statewise_gdp.html.

Auroville. (2010). Energy from the Sun. Retrieved December 10, 2010 from http://www.auroville.org/research/ren_energy/solar.htm

Das, Dr. Nachiketa. (2008). Harnessing Solar Energy in Orissa. Retrieved on October 8, 2010 from www.hitnews.com/harnessing_solar_energy_by_Dr_Nachiketa_Das.htm.

Kalra, P., Shekhar, R. & Shrivastava, V. (2007). Electrification and Bio-Energy Options in Rural India: India Infrastructure Report. Part I Rural Electrification. Pg. 138-177.

Jawaharlal Nehru National Solar Mission. (2010). Building Solar India: Guidelines for off-grid and decentralized solar applications and rooftop and other small solar power plants.

Kalra, Prem K., Shekhar, Rajiv and Shrivastava, Vinod K. (2007). Electrification and Bio-Energy: Options in Rural India. Part I Rural Electrification.

Karnataka Renewable Energy Development Ltd. (September 15, 2010). Renewable Energy for Clean and Sustainable Development: Solar Photovoltaic, Wind Energy, Small Hydro and Bio Gasifier. Bureau of Energy Efficiency: Ministry of Power, Government of India.

Gandhi, Dr. S., Singh, Dr. D.P. et al. (2009). Mumbai Human Development Report. Oxford University Press.

Grey, Mary. (2005). Dalit Women and the Struggle for Social Justice in a World of Global Capitalism. The Journal of the British and Ireland School of Feminist Theology. Sage Publications LTD.

India on a Page. (2009). Orissa. http://www.indiaonapage. com/India/Orissa/ Business /Banks /2/item.htm.

International Energy Agency (IEA). (2010). Retrieved November 22, 2010 from   http://www.iea.org/.

International Labour Organization. (2006). Global child labour trends 2000 to 2004. Geneva: Statistical Information and Monitoring on Child labour (SIMPOC) and International Program on the Elimination of Child Labour (IPEC). Retrieved July 2, 2009.

Jena, Manipadma. (2010). Environment-India: Law on Forest Rights Fails to Deliver.   GALDU. Resource Centre for the Rights of Indigenous Peoples. Retrieved December 3, 2010 from http://www.galdu.org/web/ index.php?odas=4397&giella1=eng

Mearns, Robin & Sinha, Saurabh. (1999). Social Exclusion and Land Administration in Orissa, India. Retrieved on February 11, 2011 from http://elibrary.worldbank.org/ content/workingpaper/10.1596/1813-9450-2124

MEDA (2006). *Solar Photovoltaic*. Retrieved on October 12, 2010 from http://www.ese. iitb.ac.in/events/ other/ renet_files/22-9/Session%203/ Implemenatation%20 of%20renewable% 20technologies(S.P.Mayabhate).pdf

Millennium Development Goals Indicators (2008). The official United Nations site for MDG indicators.

Ministry of Rural Development (2010). *Trends in Rural Development 2010*. Government of India.

Moyo, Dambisa. (2009). Dead Aid: Why Aid is not Working and How There is a Better Way for Africa.

National Informatics Centre (NIC). (2010). *National Portal of India: Literacy*. Government of India.

Ninian, A. (2008). Contemporary Review: India's untouchables; The Dalits. Vol. 290.

Organization for Economic Cooperation and Development. Development Cooperation Directorate (DCD-DAC) The Paris Declaration and AAA. (2008). Retrieved August 9, 2010 from the World Wide Web: http://www.oecd.org/ document/ 18/0, 3343, en_2649_3236398_3540 1554_1_1_1_1, 00.html

Orissa Energy Department. Budget Plan. (2009). Retrieved on September 8, 2010 from http://www.rtiorissa.gov.in/Department/Energy/4.

Orissa Human Development Report. (2004). P & C Department, Government of Orissa.

Pan, Jiahua and Peng, Wuyuan. (2006). Rural Electrification in China: History and Institution. China & World Economy: 71-84, Vol. 14, No. 1. Retrieved December 12, 2010 from http://iis-db.stanford.edu/pubs/22224/b Rural_Electrification_China_ Peng.

Pawar, U. (2006). The story that was my life. India's caste system reduces its untouchables to a less-than -human-status. Two Dalits tell their stories in recently published books.

Power-Technology. (2011). Solar Tower, Seville, Spain. Retrieved on January 14, 2011 from http://www.

power-technology.com/projects/Seville-Solar-Tower/
    specs.html.

Rai, V. & Simon, L. (2008). Think India. New York, USA:
    Penguin Group.

Rajiv Gandhi Grameen Vidyutikaran Yojana. (2010). Scheme
    for Rural Electricity Infrastructure and Household
    Electrification. Rural Electrification Corporation Ltd.
    Ministry of Power. Government of India. Retrieved
    on October 23, 2010 from http://rggvy.gov.in/rggvy/
    rggvyportal/index.html.

Saswati Das and Diganta Mukherjee. (2008). Role of
    Parental Education in Child Labour Decision: Urban
    India in the Last Decade. Vol. 89 Issue 2, p305-322.

SELCO-India. (2010). Energy Access Initiative Concept
    Paper.

Seth, Suman. (2009). Multidimensional Inequality
    Measurement. Retrieved on February 4, 2011 from
    http://www.ophi.org.uk/wp-content/uploads/
    Multidimensional- Inequality_SS.pdf.

Sharma, A. (2005). Dr. B. R. Ambedkar on the Aryan
    invasion and the emergence of the caste system in
    India.

Solar PV options for Rural Electrification. (2010).

Solar Energy Centre. (2010). National Renewable Energy
    Company. India Solar Resource   Maps. Retrieved
    on November 12, 2010 from http://www.nrel.gov/
    international/ ra_india.html.

Solar India Online. (2009). Analysis Securities Pvt Ltd.
    Retrieved on Novemeber 21, 2010 from http://www.
    solarindiaonline.com/profile.html.

SPARC (2004-05). SPARC annual report. Retrieved on
    October 3, 2009 from www.sparcindia.org

TCINDIA. (2008). State map of Orissa. Retrieved on October 04, 2010 from http://www. tcindia.com/maps/orissa.html

The Carbon Neutral Company. (2010). Dhulia Wind Power. Retrieved on November 25, 2010 from http://www.carbonneutral.com/project-portfolio/dhulia-wind-power/

UNDP. (2008). Human Development Indices: A Statistical Update 2008-HDI Rankings. Retrieved June 16, 2009 from: http://hdr.undp.org/en/statistics/

UNDP. (2010). International Human Development Indicators. Retrieved December 10, 2010 from http://hdrstats.undp.org/en/tables/default.html.

World Bank (2011). Energy Access. Retrieved March 3, 2011 from http://web.worldbank.org/WBSITE/EXTERNAL/NEWS/0,contentMDK:21328449~pagePK:64257043~piPK:437376~theSitePK:4607,00.html

World Health Organization (2008). Accelerating progress towards achieving maternal and child health Millennium Development Goals (MGDs) 4 and 5 in South-East Asia: Report of a high level consultation. Retrieved on October 4, 2009 from http://www.searo.who.int/LinkFiles/FCH_SEA-CHD-7

ILO. (2006). *Global Child Labour Trends 2000 to 2004*. Geneva: Statistical Information and Monitoring on Child Labour (SIMPOC) and International Program on the Elimination of Child Labour (IPEC). Retrieved July 2, 2009. http://www.ilo.org/ipecinfo/product/viewProduct.do?productId=2299 http://www.ilo.org/public/english/region/asro/newdelhi/ipec/responses/action/index.htm

Saswati Das and Diganta Mukherjee. (2008). Role of Parental Education in Child Labour Decision:

Urban India in the Last Decade. Vol. 89 Issue 2, p305-322.

Rai, V. & Simon, L. (2008). *Think India*. New York, USA: Penguin Group.

UNESCO. (2009). *Education for all: human right and catalyst for development*. Retrieved May 28, 2009 from: http://www.unesco.org/education/gmr2009/press/ efagmr2009_Chapter1.pdf

Appendices

Appendix 1: Electrical Production, Consumption, Expenditures, HDI

USD (2009)	Electrical production 2009 (KwH)	Consumption (2007)	Total Loss (KwH)	Educational Expenditure	HDI (182 Countries)
India	723,800,000,000 (6)	568,000,000,000	155,800,000,000	3.2%	119
USA	4,110,000,000,000 (1)	3,873,000,000,000	237,000,000,000	5.3%	4
China	3,451,000,000,000 (2)	3,438,000,000,000	13,000,000,000	1.9%	92
Japan	957,900,000,000 (5)	925,500,000,000	32,400,000,000	3.5%	10
Italy	289,700,000,000 (14)	315,000,000,000	-25,300,000,000	4.5%	18
Australia	239,900,000,000 (17)	222,000,000,000	17,900,000,000	4.5%	2

Appendix 3: Rural energy access of Indian Villages

	State Name	Date of Issue	Number of Unelectrified Villages	Number of Unelectrified Hamlets	Total:
1	Jarkhand	2006	19,737	66,553	86,290
2	Uttar Pradesh	2010	28,726	38,383	67,109
3	Orissa	2005	17,895	42,429	60,324
4	Bihar	2005	23,211	30,515	53,726
5	Assam	2010	4438	27,806	32,244
6	Uttarakhand	2010	787	20,381	21,168
7	Chhattisgarh	2010	772	15,413	16,185
8	Andra Pradesh	2010		14,334	14,334
9	Maharashtra	2010		4768	4768
10	Arunanchal Pradesh	2010	1788	205	1993
11	Manipur	2010	438	888	1326
			Total villages: 97,792 Total costs to. electrify: $23,470,080	Total hamlets: 261,693 Total costs to electrify: $62,806,320	Total: 359,485 Total costs: $86,276,400,000 2.4% of Indian GDP

(RGGVY, 2010)

Appendix 7: All Unelectrified and Electrified Districts in Orissa.

Top 5 Orissan Districts (High HDI)	District Name	Un-Electrified	Electrified	Total:
1.	Khorda	94	1120	1341
2.	Jharsuguda	16	305	348
3.	Cuttack	15	1693	1854
4.	Sundargarh	641	883	1758
5.	Debagarh	338	317	683
Orissan Districts with Lowest HDI				
6.	Malklanagiri,	761	156	958
7.	Kandhamal	1416	755	2359
8.	Gajapati	633	746	1510
9.	Koraput	1262	579	1858
10.	Nabarangpur	421	350	898

Endnotes

Part 1

[1] The International Poverty Line of $1.25 (PPP US) is a benchmark derived from the national poverty rates of 15 countries. For India, the national poverty line is set at $1.02 (PPP US) per day (World Bank, 2011, para. 2-5).

[2] Disproportionate rates of hunger and malnutrition are reported from India's rural regions and within the scheduled tribes (Shiva & Jalees, 2009, p. 44).

[3] India has a literacy rate of 63.8% (HDI, 2010, Country Profile:India)

[4] Climactic changes has resulted in drastic weather patterns in northern India. The 2010 monsoon season generated unprecedented flooding in Ladakh and the state of Uttarakhand. Both regions suffered the vast destruction of commercial, farm and residential land. The loss of farm land and crops has placed increasing pressure on the price of food as staple food supplies decline.

[5] The increasing cost of fossil fuels has in part translated to the inflated cost of staple foods in India. Pushing the cost of food beyond the threshold in which low-income families can afford, the Government of India was led to a decision to procure five million tones of subsidised rice and wheat for the Targeted Public Distribution System and to ban all exports from India on pulses until 2012 (RBI, 2010, para, 10; USDA, 2010, p. 4).

[6] Vanessa Louise Goodall, Food Security and India, Masters Research Project

Part 2

[1]   Genesis. The Holy Bible. New Testament.

[2]   -Sri Guru Granth Sahib Ji. Guru Nanak Dev Ji.

[3]   -Sri Guru Granth Sahib Ji. Guru Gobind Singh Ji. Tenth Sikh Guru. Guru Gobind Singh Ji introduced the five K's in order to protect Sikhs from unjust treatment within India and the world and to preserve the Sikh way. The five K's include: the Kara (iron bracelet), Khesh (unshorn hair), Kanga (comb), Kashara (loin cloth), Kirpaan (protective sword).

[4]   -Sri Guru Granth Sahib Ji (Page 1231 Line 3). Raag Sarang: The Fifth Guru. Guru Arjan Dev Ji composed the Sri Guru Granth Sahib Ji—The Sikh Holy book, now revered as the living Guru of the Sikhs.

[5]   -Sri Guru Granth Sahib Ji (Pg. 96 Translation). Guru Nanak Dev Ji. First Sikh Guru (Teacher) of the philiosophies associated with Sikhism—a spiritual way of life unnamed by religion. The main tenants of Sikhism as Guru Nanak introduced them: Honest work, sharing what you have earned with others, equality of all man kind, living in contentment and high spirits—the highest principle of Sikhism is the reality that God exists in every place. He is all knowing, all seeing and His presence is everlasting.

[6]   -Sri Guru Granth Sahib Ji (Pg. 96 Translation). Guru Nanak Dev Ji.

[7]   -Sri Guru Granth Sahib Ji. Guru Nanak Dev Ji.

[8]   -Sri Guru Granth Sahib Ji. Guru Nanak Dev Ji.

About the Author

Gurpavan Kaur Gill is a teacher with the Vancouver School Board. She has a Master of Arts in Human Security and Peace-building, and she has conducted development work and research on solar energy and human rights in Africa, India, China, and Canada. She has also travelled extensively throughout Europe and America, studying art and art history. Gurpavan continues to paint and write poetry in Vancouver, British Columbia, where she now resides.